Front cover image supplied
by Porto Zante Villas

Produced by:
Quintessentially Publishing Ltd.
29 Portland Place. London. UK. W1B 1QB
☎ +44 (0)203 073 6845
✉ production@quintessentiallypublishing.com
🌐 www.quintessentiallypublishing.com

Design by:
The Design Surgery Ltd.
13 Emmott Road. London. UK. E1 4QN
☎ +44 (0)7940 283 570
✉ studio@thedesignsurgery.co.uk
🌐 www.thedesignsurgery.co.uk

WELCOME

Welcome to Quintessentially Reserve 2012, the sixth edition of our guide to a collection of the world's most exclusive, luxurious hotels and holiday retreats. As always, we scour the globe, from the plains of Africa to the sunny beaches of Florida, from the historically rich cities of Europe to the exotic islands of the Pacific. You'll gasp at the luxury safari lodges, amble through great chateaux and manors, pad contentedly along pristine private beaches, and swim in crystal-clear waters.

The 2012 edition sees a shift in editorial content and approach. We have focused on the magic of travel and, in some cases, called upon a hand-picked selection of world-class travel journalists.

And thus, for the first time, Quintessentially Reserve will be filling the shelves of some of the most prestigious stores in the world, cementing its place at the very peak of the luxury travel book genre. It will also be available online and as an e-book. Wherever you are, whoever you're with and with any destination in mind, you can see the world through the eyes of Quintessentially Reserve and its team of magnificent writers. It will transport you immediately into your wildest dreams and fantasies – except, in this instance, the dreams come true. They say you should always make a list of 100 things to see and experience in your lifetime. Put that pen down and look no further – we have a list of unmissable destinations for you.

Christopher Rayner
Managing Director

Nathalie Grainger
Head of Editorial

Tom Parker
Project Manager

LUXURY LIFESTYLE PUBLICATIONS

EXCLUSIVE COLLECTIONS
WHITE LABELLING
BESPOKE BOOKS
CONSULTANCY

QUINTESSENTIALLY
PUBLISHING

QUINTESSENTIALLY TRAVEL GROUP

YOUR TAILOR-MADE PASSPORT TO THE WORLD

Baros Maldives Resort & Spa

IF YOU COULD BE ANYWHERE IN THE WORLD, WHERE WOULD IT BE?

A remote paradise island, a desert oasis, a mountain-top retreat? Or do you need to be inspired? Whatever your wish, the masters of travel couture are here to deliver the most hip, stylish and quintessential experience imaginable.

So whether it is a city, safari or sun getaway you choose, we will tailor your holiday the world over. We will be on hand to offer divine guidance, and cater to your every whim and desire, from the moment you plan your trip to the moment you return - and everything in-between.

Of course, we will also make sure you arrive in style, be it by private or commercial jet, a luxury chauffeur-driven car or even on the back of an Indian elephant. From the ordinary to the extraordinary, the known to the unknown, we don't just create holidays, we create experiences that last a lifetime.

www.quintessentiallytravel.com

info@quintessentiallytravel.com

LONDON	**NEW YORK**	**HONG KONG**	**DUBAI**	**GENEVA**
+44 (0)845 269 1152	+1 212 206 6633	+852 2540 8595	+971 4 437 6802	+41 (0)840 313 313

CONTENTS

EUROPE

The Croquet Lawn at
Chewton Glen luxury country
house hotel and spa

Above
Vetiver Restaurant: appealing
and perfect for every occasion

Top right
Delightful Junior Suites come
in modern or traditional styles

Bottom right
Indoor Swimming Pool
at the award-winning spa

CHEWTON GLEN HOTEL

HAMPSHIRE, ENGLAND
COORDINATES: Ⓝ 50° 44' 44.7822" Ⓦ 1° 40' 53.3922"

As you approach Chewton Glen, with its sweeping manicured lawns and well kept gardens, Agatha Christie thrillers and *Brideshead Revisted* are called to mind. Located on the edge of the New Forest, a ten-minute walk from the sea, this 18th-century house, remodelled in the 1890s, retains its charm and provides the quintessentially modern English luxury experience. Think traditional English afternoon tea, overlooking the croquet lawn, and pre-dinner gin and tonics in the Colonel Tinker's Bar.

Yet, happily, the stuffiness you may expect from a classic hotel is not part of the experience and ambience here. From the moment you arrive, you are made to feel utterly welcome and relaxed by the genuinely friendly staff. Striking the perfect balance, service is not intrusive, but always attentive and helpful, whatever the request. This personalised attention to detail is echoed throughout the property, from the pre-stamped postcards in your room ready for writing, to the wellington boots by the front door

for exploring the nearby woodland and the bicycles available for the short ride to the beach at sunset
Aside from the wonderful setting, the sublime spa with its enormous swimming pool and high ceiling, painted with a night sky complete with stars, and the mouthwatering locally sourced English cuisine, which initially entice you to stay at Chewton Glen, it is without question the fantastic team and superb service that will encourage you to return time and again.

Top left
The striking black mosaic indoor pool at Sequoia spa

Bottom left
The Blue Lounge in the heart of the mansion

Above
A bed with a view over the expansive grounds

THE GROVE

HERTFORDSHIRE, ENGLAND
COORDINATES: Ⓝ 51° 40' 38.2296" Ⓦ 0° 26' 11.7126"

The Grove, often referred to as London's country estate, is much more than a five-star hotel coveted by royalty and dignitaries. Surrounded by 300 acres of rolling Hertfordshire countryside and only 18 miles from London's Hyde Park Corner, it's also a luxury 18-hole golf resort and a fabulous Sequoia spa, complete with indoor and outdoor pools, therapeutic vitality treatments, its own urban beach and sumptuous relaxation rooms. There are three restaurants, each with its own bar – the sophisticated Colette's, with stunning views over Charlotte's Vale, The Glasshouse, buzzing with chefs working in the kitchen, and The Stables, serving excellent and simple food in a family-friendly atmosphere.

Dating back to the late-18th century, The Grove has been lovingly and tastefully restored to stunning effect. The property fuses contemporary design and original period architecture with exceptionally caring and professional service to revolutionise your English country-house experience. Some places really do need to be seen to be believed.

A championship golf
course in a breath-taking
setting at The Grove

10
11
12
13
14
15
16
17
18
19
20
21
22
23

ENGLAND

Top left
The Donovan Bar pays homage to photographer Terence Donovan

Bottom left
The Deluxe King Mansard Room offers well-appointed contemporary comfort

Above
Classic Suites are elegant, stylish, welcoming and ideal for families

ROCCO FORTE BROWN'S HOTEL

LONDON, ENGLAND
COORDINATES: Ⓝ 51° 30' 32.8458" Ⓦ 0° 8' 32.2362"

Brown's Hotel is one of the most stylish addresses in London. Nestled in the heart of Mayfair, it has, since its opening as London's first hotel in 1837, been a fashionable hotspot for opinion leaders and celebrities, from Winston Churchill and Rudyard Kipling to David Cameron and Stella McCartney. Everyone is a VIP here though. The hotel's concierge team will make you feel utterly at home – being able to choose your perfect pillow is a lovely touch.

After a trip round the West End boutiques – Bond Street and Regent Street are just minutes away – the hotel's award-winning afternoon tea is just the ticket with a selection of teas, sumptuous sandwiches and freshly-baked cakes. There's a complimentary sample of tea to take away that completes this quintessentially English experience. Renowned for its sense of innovation and taste, the hotel celebrates world-class cuisine against a backdrop of jaw-dropping British art. HIX at The Albemarle showcases work from Tracey Emin and Michael Landy – a stunning setting for a dining experience – while The Donovan Bar pays homage to iconic photographer

Terence Donovan, dedicating a "naughty corner" to a series of his more risque prints.

Despite its sleek and sophisticated lines, this hotel is family-friendly with activities and facilities to enable everyone to enjoy the experience – inter-connecting rooms and kids' TV programmes, for example.

The hotel's motto – Once a guest of Brown's, always a guest of Brown's – echoes in your mind long after checking out. Make no mistake, it's the only place to be – and be seen.

CLARIDGE'S

LONDON, ENGLAND
COORDINATES: Ⓝ 51° 30' 45.6762" Ⓦ 0° 8' 51.522"

Claridge's, minutes from the chic boutiques of Bond Street in the heart of Mayfair, truly deserves to be known as the art deco jewel in London's crown. Staff greet you with touching politeness and pride themselves on the personal touch. The doorman will remember each and every guest, and the team go to great lengths to anticipate your every need.

There's an overwhelming feeling of wellbeing as you walk through the elegant revolving doors into the Front Hall. You enter a timelessly glamorous world where the tinkling of piano music in the Foyer gives way to the gentle chink of Martini glasses in Claridge's Bar. This seriously stylish venue sees London's movers and shakers rub shoulders with royalty while sipping flamboyant cocktails and fine champagnes. The elegant grandeur of the 1930s is done great justice in the sumptuous Fumoir where gentlemen and ladies retire for a well-earned night cap.

If you cherish your creature comforts, you're in for a treat. Each room and suite mixes modern and traditional design, and offers space and tranquillity. There's also a fabulous gym and a spa tucked away on the 6th floor for exceptional pampering treatments. Elsewhere you can relax and enjoy the award-winning afternoon tea served in the Foyer or sample the contemporary seasonal menu in the Reading Room. This extraordinary hotel takes luxurious pleasures very seriously – the Royal Family refers to it as the Annexe to Buckingham Palace and we can't say fairer than that.

Above
The Fumoir serves Thirties-themed cocktails in style

Top right
The Linley Suite has been beautifully restored by design company Linley

Bottom right
One of the Piano Suite's two glamorous bedrooms

CORINTHIA HOTEL LONDON

LONDON, ENGLAND
COORDINATES: Ⓝ 51° 30' 23.8392" Ⓦ 0° 7' 25.8528"

It claims to be the latest London legend in the making. Indeed, satisfied guests have already judged this newly refurbished landmark hotel an "instant classic". Frédérique Andreani checked in to find out for herself

Top left
The Trafalgar Suite enjoys views of Trafalgar Square and Nelson's Column

Bottom left
Contemporary luxury of the Trafalgar Suite bedroom: modern style in historic London

Right
The Lobby Whitehall Entrance blends classical architecture with the coolest modern art

Even before visiting the Corinthia, which first opened in 1885 as the Metropole, I am already conquered by its ornate golden sandstone exterior, which reminds me of the Haussmanian apartment blocks of my native Paris. I am also already impressed by its rich heritage. Indeed, I have read how the prestigious hotel, located a few minutes' walk from Trafalgar Square, used to be a favourite of transatlantic adventurers, colonial visitors and aristocrats alike. I also know that the hotel was beloved by Edward VII, who kept a suite here, and am aware of its reputation as one of the Season's favourite addresses during the Roaring Twenties. So this is in a state of both anticipation and daydream that I first pass its entrance, mentally picturing some of Nancy Mitford's rosy debutantes here to attend their first ball.

Indeed, on entering the hotel, it is easy to imagine some bright young things in pearls and party gear gallivanting among the dramatic Calacatta marble columns, oak-timbered walls, comfortable leather furniture and silk cushions. While there are no debutantes to be seen, the lobby is, however, populated with a rather glamorous crowd, mostly made up of designers, journalists and models attending London Fashion Week shows, which were taking place at nearby Somerset House. But, despite its five-star status, the hotel's mood is welcoming rather than formal, conveying an obvious sense of luxury but without the often-attached ostentation, which makes me feel instantly at ease rather than self-conscious.

Indeed, the Corinthia displays none of the over-stuffy decor that often characterises this type of historic grand hotel. Airy, spacious and inundated with natural light, its elegance is instead left to breathe. And, while three years of meticulous work have succeeded in restoring the building's former glory, some striking contemporary features signal that its new owners clearly wish to avoid too much nostalgia. The building might be clearly proud of its heritage, but its sense of style is also firmly steeped in the 21st century, like some sort of Victorian dream gone modern.

The Full Moon, a 4.15-metre crystal chandelier under the atrium dome of the Lobby Lounge, is a case in point. Created by Parisian designer Chafik Gasmi and produced by Baccarat, this lustre is composed of 1,001 crystal baubles, with one signature, single red crystal lying at its heart. The biggest of its kind, this sculptural piece infuses a shot of 21st-century design at its best to the hotel's 19th-century beauty. I am struck, during my visit to the Corinthia, by the attention to detail, such as the lobby lift doors decorated with metal casts of leaves taken from the parks around the hotel. Guests can also admire exquisite floral arrangements made of delicate country roses, displayed like mini sculptures in simple glass vases and conveying a sense of understated, arty chic. The Harrods Room is also worthy of note. Small but perfectly formed,

The Lobby Lounge is an iconic space illuminated in grand style

this outpost of the otherwise gigantic London store evokes a charming 19th-century tea room, where old-fashioned quality is cleverly offset by super-modern, bright-blue chandeliers. On the evening I spend there, the elegant Northall restaurant, which specialises in the best of seasonal British, was hosting an event attracting a fashionable crowd of guests. I had a drink at its bar and, despite its impressive design, I get the sense that the hotel doesn't take itself too seriously. This is a place which wants its guests to enjoy themselves, to relax or have fun rather than pose.

After my brief stay among the fashionistas, I make my way to the hotel destination bar for a taste of its innovative molecular cocktails. While The Northall is bright and spacious, the much quieter Bassoon exudes a dark and glamorous sexiness fit for a secret rendezvous, with its snug banquettes of silvery leather and intimate atmosphere. With my weakness for experimental cocktails, I am pleasantly surprised by the wide choice and eventually settle for the Bubblegum Martini. A liquid feast for the eyes as well as the palate, the utterly delicious concoction is elegantly adorned with a fresh rose petal, and made from marshmallow infused vodka and bubblegum foam. Sipping at it, I am instantly transported into childhood nostalgia, albeit with some very sophisticated undertones. The taste is comforting, sweet but not syrupy, and very original – undoubtedly one of the best cocktails I'd ever had, which put me in a good mood to admire the decor. Here, the style is resolutely Art Deco rather than Victoriana, therefore evoking the second life of the Hotel Metropole, when it was taken over by the Government to be used by the Ministry of Defence, and most notably by Winston Churchill, during the Second World War. The walls are covered with luxurious stingray leather, smoky mirrors and paintings evocative of the golden age of jazz, while the black lacquered bar reveals itself to be in fact the top of a seven-metre-long piano.

After promising myself to come back to Bassoon on a date, I make my way to Massimo Restaurant and Oyster Bar, opened by chef Massimo Riccioli and which is an evolved version of his much-loved Roman restaurant La Rosetta. Settling into one of the hand-stitched leather banquettes, I soon delight in a meal of scallops and super-fresh turbot, enhanced by chilled Chablis, finishing with an exquisite creme brulee. My taste buds are titillated by the zingy ginger, which manages to balance the pudding's sweetness and make it much more interesting. The space itself, designed by David Collins – of Claridge's, Wolseley and Berkeley fame – is pretty impressive. With its ten massive marble pillars, hand beaten pewter bar, giant globe lampshades, glass cabinets filled with wine bottles, oak-panelled walls and spectacular Art Nouveau mosaic, the very large room is more evocative of a glamorous Parisian brasserie than a classic Italian restaurant. On the night I visit, the atmosphere is particularly animated, with the room full of chattering foodies who are making the most of the daily sea catches. Most look like Londoners rather than tourists – not that the latter are bad, of course, especially in a hotel restaurant – but the fact that it has an authentic London feel wins a brownie point.

When the time comes to go to sleep, I am not disappointed by my bedroom either, both spacious at 45 square metres and bathed in natural light. Despite opening onto the busy street, the place is surprisingly quiet and feels like a welcoming cocoon. Declined in a palette of beige colours, from the shantung silk that covers the wall behind the bed to the velvet sofa and blond wood floor, it evokes warmth rather than blandness. Here the decoration is resolutely Art Deco, with 1930s touches such as chrome lamps and an elegant marble-topped mini bar. However, contemporary comfort is paramount, with modern gadgets like a Nespresso machine – a great touch for a coffee-holic like myself – or the "hot box" I find in the morning with my breakfast and which cleverly keeps my cappuccino and croissants warm. The same goes for the glamorous bathroom. With its giant round mirror and white marble floors and features, it reminds me both of the golden age of Hollywood and of the most languorous hammams I visited in Turkey, albeit with a plasma TV over the bath and a powerful rain shower. So it is well rested that I conclude my stay the day after at the ESPA Life at Corinthia, the hotel's magnificent – and gigantic – spa. Spread over four floors and covering 3,300

Harrods and florist
Ercole Moroni have
outlets in the hotel

square metres, it leads the visitor
from modernist white in its lobby
to opulent darkness. There again, I
am struck by the chosen materials,
which include black marble, lacquer
panels, dark oak, polished chrome
and textured leather, to create a
space which is contemporary yet
sumptuous. After a tailored 80-minute
back-and-scalp massage, which is
both efficient in releasing muscle
pain but relaxing enough to plunge
me in a heavenly state of bliss, I am
left to wander around the spa. And I
make the most of its facilities, such
as the very contemporary silver steel
swimming pool, the vitality pool with
water massage jets, the several black
mosaic steam rooms, the amphitheatre
sauna and its nearby ice fountain, and
the heated relaxation beds situated
opposite ambient fireplaces. An
independent Daniel Galvin hair salon
is conveniently located within the spa,
to ensure that guests can experience
the ultimate blow-dry after their visit.
Visiting celebs and privileged clients
can even get pampered at the Ultimate
Make-Over Room, the brainchild of
Oscar-winning make-up artist Lois
Burwell, which offers total privacy and
unparalleled luxury.

It's fully rested, pampered, well-fed
and relaxed that I eventually leave
the Corinthia. Re-entering the busy
West End gives me a slight shock after
the opulent peace found within the
hotel, where – in words borrowed
from French poet Charles Baudelaire –
"everything seems about luxury, calm
and voluptuous delight".

The Schiaparelli Suite is named after the designer who unleashed fuchsia on a glamour-starved world

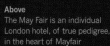

Above
The May Fair is an individual London hotel, of true pedigree, in the heart of Mayfair

Top right
Studio Suites are elegantly designed with a work desk, lounge area and latest technology

Bottom right
Quince restaurant is the perfect expression of chef patron Silvena Rowe's exuberant personality

ENGLAND

THE MAY FAIR HOTEL

LONDON, ENGLAND
COORDINATES: Ⓝ 51° 30' 29.3538" Ⓦ 0° 8' 37.3668"

When staying in a city like London, the choice of hotels can be a little bewildering. The focus is generally on accessibility, comfort and good service. Luxury, sought after by discerning guests, is a bonus. The May Fair Hotel offers just that – five-star luxury in the heart of Mayfair, within minutes of Green Park, fabulous shopping and London's West End.

As you wander through the glamorous lobby, or people-watch in the cool atmosphere of the bar, it's easy to see why this veritable institution has consistently attracted Hollywood stars and world leaders, right back to its opening in 1927.

The hotel is known for its excellent staff-to-client rapport. The team are attentive to your every need, so be sure to take advantage of the 24-hour concierge service for any special requirements you may have.

There are touches of genius everywhere. The hotel boasts 12 of the most memorable London suites which alone are worth the stay, one of London's largest private theatres and Europe's biggest privately commissioned Baccarat chandelier.

The fashionable May Fair Bar is not only renowned for its dazzling menu of more than 40 signature cocktails, it also incorporates the legendary 150 at the May Fair, an exclusive enclave which is a luxe magnum bar serving the finest champagnes.

Quince at the May Fair is a destination in its own right and is a superior Eastern Mediterranean eatery inspired by one of the world's oldest cuisines. And the serene May Fair Spa hits the mark for urban pampering after a long walk around the shops.

SHANGRI-LA HOTEL, PARIS

PARIS, FRANCE
COORDINATES: (N) 48° 51' 49.8384" (E) 2° 17' 36.0708"

An exclusive, if eclectic, residence fit for a French emperor is now one of the most luxurious hotels in Paris and attracts discerning, if curious, visitors from around the world, as Josh Sims discovers

The young Asian woman playing the piano during afternoon tea could be another Lang Lang, although Lang Lang probably doesn't do much in the way of jazzy covers of *Like A Virgin*. Situated under the glass cupola of the Shangri-La Hotel, Paris, the tinkling Madonna fan embodies the quirky contradictions of the hotel group's first foray into the European market – and it's something of a grand entrance at that.

In one restaurant, there's fancy chef-work of the kind that only the French really appreciate – every dish an edible sculpture, each ingredient fighting to move on from its humble roots and be a star. Another menu allows you to dive into a bowl of spaghetti with a side of strawberry milkshake and a terribly fashionable cupcake to follow.

Rooms have postcard views that look out onto the Eiffel Tower and yet are so plush and textural and touchy-feely on the inside that you barely remember to look out of the window. Staff remember your name – more than that, they even remember where you sat for breakfast yesterday and ask if you want the same seat – and show a willingness to help bordering on an obsessive compulsion and yet are relaxed enough to share a joke about it all.

"Can I take your bag?" a porter asks me, not really meaning it as a question. "If you like," I reply, about to explain that, a grown man, I can handle such a small, overnight bag myself. "Please," he implores. "It's my job..." Smiles all round – and that uncomfortable role play of upstairs and below stairs, which top hotels sometimes painfully force on staff and guests alike, disappears in an instant.

That is some relief when one visits a place so palatial. Certainly many hotels might make a claim to such an adjective, seeking to describe the sweep of the foyer, the luxuriousness of the materials, maybe even the butler-like demeanor of the staff, especially given that at the Shangri-La there are, the management says, four members of staff for every guest – that's one to bring you each of the versions of the Pink Lady cocktail available on the bar menu. But the Shangri-La on Avenue d'Iéna can use said adjective with precision. The building was, in fact, the residence of Prince Roland Bonaparte until his death in 1924. Here was a man with a surname that nodded to France's imperial past, (Roland was Napoleon's grandnephew), with a taste in decoration that matched: high

vaults – double, triple, quadruple-height ceilings – and precious materials, marble that glistens and staircases that, of course, sweep. The French reputation as a culture-loving people also took some battering during the building's lifetime. After Roland's family sold the property, various owners had done their best to turn a fantasy interior into something akin to a corporate training room. Parquet flooring was carpeted over, mahogany-lined rooms slathered in grey or, what seems stranger, electric-blue paint and the steel structure supporting that cupola – one built a couple of years after the opening of Eiffel's tower and with a clear reference to its industrial powerhouse aesthetic – had been boxed in, something no one has yet attempted with the tower at least. The Shangri-La Group bought the property and, even if the resulting hotel had been terrible, its masterful restoration job would have to be applauded. And it has been. In 2009, the former Palais Iéna was awarded listed status by Monuments Historiques, the institution that deals with such matters in France.

Many hotels around the world may be impressive in their own way. But very few warrant a visit even by those who live locally, or who are staying at other hotels, just to catch a glimpse of how the other half lived during the second part of the 19th century. Entering the Shangri-La is still like entering someone's home – if that someone just happens to be related to an emperor. Look closely, in fact, and the wooden relief work features the bee, Roman armory, lions' heads and giant eagles – all Napoleonic symbols. But the restoration work has been completed so seamlessly, what is original – the 1,000 panels of parquet flooring taken up, cleaned and put down again – and what is modern – the 8,000 pieces of gold leaf applied liberally throughout the interior – becomes impossible for all, but an expert, to discern. This interior, as befits the hotel's owners, has something of an Asiatic touch to it. Bird motifs and crimson upholstery, black lacquer and ornate

rugs all hint of the Far East, even if seen through the prism of western influence, with chandeliers made out of Murano glass and windows in period stained glass. One could be quick to call it a hotchpotch, where the occident and orient collide. It suggests the wealthy, very well-to-do man of the late-1800s and his interest in taking in the world as part of his on-going self-education, collecting and cataloguing along the way. Here's a statue of a fat little boy holding a cornucopia-cum-light picked up on some jaunt, there another of an Egyptian negress, there a giant Ming-like vase, there a print of some exotic plant or a hint of something Grecian. And behind the concierge's desk there is a huge cabinet full of huge plates, no doubt once used to serve hugely exotic dishes. Roland spared nothing on the masonry – his master masons were Steiner and Houguenade, who also worked on the Louvre and the Tuileries Palace. But he also spared nothing when it came to filling the spaces in between either. Indeed, he did so out of his passions – geography, geology, ethnology – that gave rise to the world's largest private herbarium, a treasure trove of Napoleonic memorabilia (well, you can't shake the family tree) and a collection of 200,000 books over six kilometres of shelving, which perhaps explains why he didn't look for a more bijou abode when it came to setting up home in Paris. The resulting interior style, which the restorers have honoured, is almost inevitably an eclectic one. It was so even in Roland's day. Blending the 17th and 19th centuries, they even called it the Eclectic Style – and that was perhaps the only unoriginal thing about it. Small wonder the Palais became something of a salon – in the intellectual rather than the hairstyling sense – for the great and good of the day. Certainly, for all that, the four-year-long restoration is essentially historic. It, of course, looks to a viewpoint that, at its time, was modern and progressive. And, crucially, the Shangri-La Hotel, Paris may seem like

a large and unwieldy time-travelling machine, but doesn't feel like a museum – more so simply a place replete with detail. The rooms are like miniature versions of the whole – lush and tactile – with that quirky mix of styles, but not forgoing the essentials even Roland had to live without – the walk-in shower, decadently big enough for four, let alone two; a TV with (oh rare joy!) a channel selection that recognises one might want more entertainment in English than the standard BBC World allows; and, better still, a proper, help-yourself coffee machine, recognising that even those unfortunate individuals who prefer to maintain that certain upstairs-below stairs hauteur towards hotel staff may sometimes not want to go through the rigmarole of calling room service. There is even a pot of jasmine tea waiting, warm in a wicker basket, by the bed to ease each guest's arrival. Elsewhere, there are the usual services too – the gym which, like most hotel gyms, is quiet and still, its hefty sweat machines standing monolithically and unused; and, much more appealing, the hotel's latest addition, the swimming pool and what the Shangri-La management prefers to call a Wellness Area.

They do the rest of the hotel a disservice in doing so, for its lounges, rooms and restaurants are no less wellness areas in their own way. Certainly some people seem to feel very comfortable here. There is the guy in one of the foyer's capacious reception rooms, who seems to make his cake and copy of *Le Monde* last a supernaturally long time. There is the arty couple with their kids – beautiful and stylish as only French children seem capable of being – who while away a peaceful, long lunch, only occasionally looking askance at my spaghetti and milkshake combo. There is the loving couple – alone in the bar, with the exception of the barman and waiter, politely busying themselves polishing already sparkling glasses – who seem determined to swallow each other. Like any other hotel, it brings all sorts together, for all sorts of reasons. Prince Roland would have approved.

Top left
The Suite Imperiale was once Roland Bonaparte's private apartment

Bottom left
The Suite Shangri-la's deck at night and a view of the Eiffel Tower

Top
The hotel offers elegant function rooms and private dining facilities

Top left
The Belle Etoile Royal
Suite terrace has a view of
the Eiffel Tower

Bottom left
The Louis XVI opulence
and comfort of a Prestige
Suite bedroom

Above
The sumptuous dining
room of haute-cuisine
Restaurant Le Meurice

LE MEURICE, THE DORCHESTER COLLECTION

PARIS, FRANCE
COORDINATES: Ⓝ 48° 51' 54.5652" Ⓔ 2° 19' 41.1492"

Le Meurice has been a definitive French luxury hotel since 1835. Basking in refined 18th-century splendour, the magic doesn't live in the past. In 2007, Philippe Starck and his daughter breathed new life into the hotel, achieving contemporary lines and elegance without altering the soul of the hotel. Charles Jouffre, hot from working on the Opera Garnier, refurbished the 160 rooms, bringing a unique touch to each, delivering atmosphere and detail, along with delightful extras such as heated bath tubs, anti-steam mirrors and iPod docking stations. As expected, dinner is a gastronomic and visual treat at Le Meurice and Le Dali restaurants. Precise and unpretentious, the three-star cuisine, devised by Chef Yannick Alléno, is groundbreaking and exquisitely presented, blending with the Philippe Starck interior.

A stay at Le Meurice is crowned by the courteous personal service of the hotel's long-serving staff who take care of you like a family member. Marvellous.

MANDARIN ORIENTAL PARIS

PARIS, FRANCE
COORDINATES: Ⓝ 48° 52' 1.74" Ⓔ 2° 19' 37.7328"

A holiday in the fashion capital of the world and city of love is truly perfect if you stay at Mandarin Oriental, Paris. Located on one of the most fashionable streets in the world, rue Saint-Honoré, this hotel lives up to the reputation and prestige of its location. Just steps away from the Louvre and world-leading fashion houses, Mandarin Oriental, Paris is the ideal location for the ultimate Parisian experience. Serenity prevails in your suite, designed to make you feel completely at home among the amazing views of the garden and monuments that line the cityscape. Although the concierge would be more than happy to help you find exquisite restaurants throughout the city, you will want to sample the haute cuisine of chef Thierry Marx. In a cocoon of exclusivity, with chic white decoration, Thierry Marx serves the best cuisine in Paris at Sur Mesure Par Thierry Marx. Another essential palate-pleaser is the Cake Shop. But, after a long day of strolling through the busy city, there is nothing to beat a delicious dessert in the garden of Camelia. Finally, you should pamper yourself at the hotel spa, which is an oasis of oriental wellbeing. With Tian Quan therapy, a Chinese bathing ritual, some holistic treatments, the 15-metre pool and water cascade, you will finish the day refreshed and ready for another Parisian outing.

Above
The courtyard garden is an oasis of calm in the bustling city centre

Top right
The Mandarin Terrace Room features chic French design and photography by Man Ray

Bottom right
The Spa and 15-metre pool are in addition to a fitness and wellness centre

The owner's passion for art is
expressed in the hotel's Lobby

Above
Modern design complements Parisian chic in Le Burgundy's Hall

Top right
The Opera Suite is an intimate retreat in the heart of the fashion district

Bottom right
Recover from the day with a swim in the beautiful turquoise pool

LE BURGUNDY PARIS

PARIS, FRANCE
COORDINATES: (N) 48° 52' 4.3206" (E) 2° 19' 32.7714"

Welcome to Le Burgundy Paris, a new jewel in the crown of good living. Oozing lightness and sophistication, the hotel captures that quintessentially Parisian mixture of sleek aesthetics and understated elegance. It's the ultimate in contemporary luxury, playing on the natural light which drenches the bright rooms and modern interiors. It is also fantastically located right in the heart of Paris on the prestigious Rue Saint-Honoré. Yet Le Burgundy is intimate, with an atmosphere of discreet elegance, despite the hustle and bustle outside. Perfect then as a base for trips to the neighbouring luxurious shopping destinations, with some of the biggest names in fashion only minutes away. What's more, Le Spa Burgundy provides the ideal post-retail-therapy relaxation, with revitalising pedicures to ease tired feet and soothing massages for those aching shoulders.

Once you're restored, make sure you don't miss the exclusive Le Baudelaire restaurant for dinner. Boasting a Michelin star, the restaurant is the epitome of modern, refined luxury, undoubtedly able to satisfy even the pickiest of gourmands with its exquisite Parisian culinary classics innovatively given an international twist. If, however, you only fancy something light, the pastry chef's creations, served in the beautiful Winter Garden, are sure to get your mouth watering. Whatever you opt for, one thing is certain, the service will be impeccable. It's friendly and efficient, giving a warm personality to this very cool hotel. Guests never fail to be charmed, which is why they come back time and time again to this outstanding boutique hotel.

Top left
Junior Suites are appointed in Louis XV and Louis XVI-style with original paintings

Bottom left
The swimming pool, decorated like a 19th-century yacht, opens out onto a rooftop sun deck

Above
The 114 Faubourg is Le Bristol's exciting new restaurant serving creative cuisine

LE BRISTOL PARIS

PARIS, FRANCE
COORDINATES: Ⓝ 48° 52' 18.2202" Ⓔ 2° 18' 53.4096"

What do you look for in a city hotel? Great location, delicious dining and comfortable rooms? Well, Le Bristol Paris ticks all the boxes. Close to the Champs-Elysees, the hotel's Head Chef Eric Frechon holds three Michelin stars – even the afternoon tea is not to be missed – and the guest rooms offer all the amenities and company. Over the years, the hotel has been popular with the likes of Charlie Chaplin, Rita Hayworth and Josephine Baker. Nothing is too much trouble, whether your request is as simple as a transfer or a theatre ticket, or more specific such as a round-trip by helicopter to Deauville or a carriage to the Opera – it will be done, swiftly

FRANCE

24
25
26
27
28
29
30
31
32
33
34
35

CASTILLE PARIS

PARIS, FRANCE
COORDINATES: Ⓝ 48° 52' 5.934" Ⓔ 2° 19' 36.6888"

If you dream of strolling down the Champs Elysées, marvelling at the Eiffel Tower and sampling delicious cuisine, then the Castille Paris may be the perfect place for you.

The hotel's location really can't be beaten. Situated in the exclusive 1st Arrondissement, the city's world-famous attractions are literally on your doorstep. The Castille sits between three historic squares and is just a short stroll away from the beautiful Tuileries Gardens. The Louvre and the Musée d'Orsay are close by too, and the neighbouring St-Germain Quarter is the perfect place to watch the fashionable world go by. Luxury fashion houses line the adjacent Rue Saint-Honoré and the world's finest jewellers display their gems on the nearby Place Vendôme. The Castille stands on the chic Rue Cambon, right next to Coco Chanel's original boutique, a Mecca for fashionistas. You'll soon discover that the elegance of the surrounding streets extends into every corner of the Castille. You'll be struck by its cosy boutique atmosphere and exceptional concierge service. Its luxurious rooms effortlessly blend Parisian and Italian styles. The Rivoli Wing pays tribute to Chanel, with a striking black, white and beige palette, while the Opera Wing is inspired by Venetian opulence – imagine silky drapes and marble bathrooms. This Italian luxury continues into the magnificent L'Assaggio Restaurant, where the head chef promises a taste of Italy in Paris. If the weather is kind, be sure to dine in the delightful Florentine courtyard, the ideal complement to the wonderful Italian cuisine .

Above
Heart of haute couture Paris where French and Italian style meet

Top right
Duplex Suites offer generous yet cosy living space on two floors

Bottom right
Dine on outstanding Italian cuisine in L'Assaggio Restaurant

Top left
Superior Rooms provide
a hushed, refined setting
decorated in Louis XV style

Bottom left
The Patio is a calm cocoon
away from the hustle and
bustle of central Paris.

Above
The Lobby of this luxury
Parisian hotel boasts
sumptuous classical decor

HOTEL DE CRILLON

PARIS, FRANCE
COORDINATES: Ⓝ 48° 52' 2.1072" Ⓔ 2° 19' 15.6606"

Few would argue that the Hotel de Crillon is the quintessence of Parisian chic. Sitting at the crossroads of world-class art and fashion, the hotel overlooks the Place de la Concorde and is just a stone's throw away from the famous Avenue des Champs-Elysees. Paris doesn't get more glamorous than this. The rooms are no exception. Adorned with marble, crystal and the plushest fabrics, the decor and style fuse Louis XV furnishings with modern-day technology.
City life can be stressful but you'd never know it here. There's a timeless elegance and poise that lend an air of serenity to the surroundings and immediately put you at ease. So exhale and pack your worries away because when it comes to wellbeing, nothing is too much trouble here. The property uses the services of world-renowned personal trainer Julie Ferrez, who looks after guests' needs and problem areas with the utmost professionalism and discretion. For lovers of beauty products par excellence, the hotel enjoys a connection with the Carita Beauty House and a comprehensive list of treatments to revive a tired complexion and weary face.
In springtime, Le Patio, a gorgeous corner of green in the city, and the recently re-opened restaurant Les Ambassadeurs are prime spots to watch the world go by and for fine dining. The resident Michelin star-winning chef Christopher Hache's culinary creations perfectly complement the grandiose design of crystal chandeliers which set off those delectable, naughty pastries. Louis XV would have asked for nothing less.

ROYAL-RIVIERA HOTEL

SAINT-JEAN-CAP-FERRAT, FRANCE
COORDINATES: Ⓝ 43° 42' 7.4226" Ⓔ 7° 19' 43.1328"

"I can resist everything except temptation." Never did Oscar Wilde's words ring truer than here, driving along the scenic Basse Corniche, drawing up in front of Hotel Royal-Riviera and catching a glimpse of the glorious gardens inspired by the great writer himself.

Being here would go down as one of life's most memorable moments. Set atop the Peninsula of Cap-Ferrat, flirting with the edges of Beaulieu, Nice and Monaco, the five-star hotel takes centre stage in the most exclusive of locations. It's the only luxury property in the region to enjoy its own private sandy beach and, if you dream of staying in an intimate private Mediterranean villa complete with the glamour of a palace, then dream no more.

As you set down your bags in one of the 94 impeccable rooms and suites, throw open the windows and breathe in the warm, fragrant air, and you immediately feel the shackles of time slipping away. As expected, the dining is exquisite at The Panorama where flavours of Provence bring sunshine to your plate. Like coming home, Royal-Riviera encourages lounging on your sea-facing balcony, reading a book in the gardens or taking in the sounds of nature without a care in the world, and in utter comfort and privacy. Entrust any requests to the exclusive concierge for that extra touch of personal service. Like the breathtaking views, the gorgeous Villa Kerylos and the sea breeze, the feelings of contentment here are priceless, lodging firmly in your memory for a lifetime.

Above
The hotel boasts a private sandy beach on the Côte d'Azur

Top right
The Suite is hugely spacious and has a large terrace

Bottom right
The luxurious terrace of a Junior Suite with Mediterranean views

GRAND-HOTEL DU CAP-FERRAT

SAINT-JEAN-CAP-FERRAT, FRANCE
COORDINATES: Ⓝ 43° 40' 36.7284" Ⓔ 7° 19' 53.3274"

Cap-Ferrat on the French Riviera has been described as paradise on Earth. Harry Hughes took a trip to paradise and experienced the pleasures of a hotel recently awarded "palace" status

The palace of light rises in beautiful silhouette, its wings open like a large dove towards the sea. My suite looks out above the conifers, and the rugged coastline stretches left to right in shades soft and alluring. I step onto the balcony and raise a toast to the setting sun. I have been here five hours and have already met two unforgettable people. The first is a girl of graceful bearing. She is pretty, German and has intimate, even passionate, knowledge of Grand-Hotel du Cap-Ferrat. "It is simple elegance that charms us," she tells me as we walk languorously through 17 acres of garden fashioned from the poetic imagination of French mastermind Jean Mus. "The hotel blends perfectly with the landscape here. It is beautiful, don't you think?" I agree and we talk like children, laughing unassumingly on our way down to Club Dauphin and the Olympic-size swimming pool that is a playground for the rich and famous. We find a mutual appreciation for the sculpture and candid architectural lines in the recently renovated spa, and I realise quickly that she has a remarkable eye for detail.
"It's a magical light here," she says

as we take a drink on the terrace and I proclaim the mastery of architect Luc Svetchine's newly appointed work that flanks the main Rotunda, originally designed by the legendary Gustave Eiffel.
"The terracotta shades work powerfully with the Aleppo trees, the blue lagoons and the pure tones of the interiors. You are quite right – it's very magical."
Then I met Brodrick. Perhaps I will never meet a man of this calibre again. The light dimming on the terrace, I stepped into the restaurant, La Veranda, where a man in linen shorts and a green wool cardigan slung over his shoulders stared back at me. I asked him where the library was and he pointed me towards a small alcove adjacent to a long, very full bar. I picked up an old book, skimmed the pages, put it back. In the mirror, I noted a large white sail boat disappear behind a wreath of cypress trees and then Brodrick appeared. On first sight, he looks like a 75-year-old ex-model. You think this because of his clothes – an accoutrement of wardrobe classics, including Ralph Lauren lace-up shoes, suede shirt and vintage leather jacket; then because of

his blue eyes that shine brighter than real life; then because of the perfect crease in his lips that only comes from holding a cigarette between his teeth since time immemorial.

"This hotel is something, I can tell you," he says, looking at me mysteriously, yet as if we already know each other. I swear we don't, but I play along, intrigued by his conversation. He puts a book back, then invites me into the bar for a Martini. It turns out Brodrick is a mathematician and sometimes an architect. I need words to describe this place, so I ask him. "Well, it's all clean lines, gliding through the pines without disturbing the serenity of the terrain," he says. "The hotel is a very classic precursor of things to come and way before its time when first built 100 years ago. It's honest, state-of-the-art and you have to have some money to make it here. Tell the layabouts to come for the spa – it's pretty darn good."

Night has fallen on the balcony and the sky is like lilac wine across the peninsula of Cap- Ferrat. I think I can hear music through the trees. I put on a clean white shirt, black trousers, solid black tie. Jack Daniels has been good company as has the lighthouse, sending out blue shimmers across my train of thought.

Downstairs, les nouvelles cuisines at the Michelin-starred Restaurant Le Cap is served. I can't find Brodrick, but there are other poetic souls on the terrace. I look around and I already know the food is good. It's written in their faces, in the way a certain gentleman leans back and whispers into the waiter's ear. The master theatre of chef Didier Aniès is alive and well, and the one Michelin star will soon become two if the goat's cheese with caramelised onions – my standard litmus test – is anything to go by.

"Food is poetic, no?" says Marion, a girl I will meet again the next day. Her open demeanour is refreshing and her black leather sandals quite charming, matched perfectly with a backless silver dress. She is sharing her cocktail with a large man in a belted cashmere

cardigan, his movements frozen by the sounds of the Mediterranean. Her eyes reflect the parade of footlights that taper down towards Club Dauphin, and her life seems quite perfect and happy in that moment.

"Let's go sailing tomorrow," she says in lilted French. He nods diffidently, just as they do in the art house movies, and the chocolate fondant and very expensive Château d'Yquem they are drinking might just be scripted for advertising potential. Behind him, a man sits at a piano and changes the atmosphere with a single gesture. Then the stream of words and wine flow free and wild, and I lean in to get my share of the beautiful sounds. I soon find out that Escoffier – king of French cuisine – is buried not far off. He too would approve of the caviar lasagne with leeks in olive oil, and so does an Italian girl with hazy green eyes, a faint sarcastic smile, a Dior handbag, and a reserved penchant for Dali and Picasso. She has spent her life wanting to live the life of Marilyn Monroe and, as I watch, she lowers her eyes suggestively and points behind her, remarking that the king-size bed in the deluxe suite in the new terra-cotta wing is just about the best thing she has ever slept in. The spa's designer Pierre-Yves Rochon is a personal friend of hers and, according to Luc Svetchine, a "true genius" who has an "exalted vision of luxury".

"After breakfast I go down to the spa and have a massage or a mud treatment," the Italian girl says. "I run outside – it's so gorgeous, looking at the sea and seeing all the people in the garden. And then I spend the rest of the time reading magazines in the Jacuzzi." She pauses, looking past me to where Brodrick suddenly appears, his enigmatic eyes searching for her, before picking us both out with that brilliant white smile.

Grand-Hotel Du Cap-Ferrat – the theme is massive, it is passionate, it will stay with me always. So will they, together with the night-time drive in the Mercedes Benz 190SL. Her emerald eyes shining like lake

Como as we carried on towards the old fishermen's quarter of La Ponche in St Tropez and his laughter along the cubist fortifications of St Paul de Vance, before my head finally dropped onto velvet in the already beloved lumiere du Cap-Ferrat.

The next morning I find myself in a room with cathedral ceilings and an open volume of Ralph Lauren. There are candelabra and silver mirrors, Parisian furniture that would work well in a Francis Ford Coppola period piece. She is there looking at me, but I don't see her until she taps me politely on the hand. I turn and her bare shoulder invites me down to Club Dauphin where all the lovers have gone that morning. We lay out our towels, I compliment her somehow and she laughs, throwing herself in the crystal lagoon. I dip my hat over a ruffled brow, watch her slowly, casually, then staring out into cloudless skies, I soon find myself in the sea.

Closer to land, where the hills throw out goodness in colours pink and cream, and Rivieran yellow, I sigh and let the pale-blue wave wash over me. On the seafront, through a private gate, there's a jetty where a couple bathe on the warm stone, sipping orange juice, smiling. They have names that remind me of the Belle Epoque. And they are kindly and rich, and know how to enjoy the company of younger, more tempestuous spirits.

Above us, the rocks climb to the hotel, its palatial facade shimmering with a quiet solitude.

Top left
Club Dauphin boasts an Olympic-sized heated sea-water swimming pool

Bottom left
The 1908 facade of the refurbished hotel, set in 17 acres of grounds

Above
The Lustre Lobby is a haven of cool French chic in the Mediterranean sun

CZECH REPUBLIC

Top left
The Charles Suite offers
spacious accommodation
and a view of Prague Castle

Bottom left
Studio Rooms have either
king-size or twin beds and
marble-lined bathrooms

Above
The Brewery Bar was once
the cellar of the original St
Thomas Brewery

ROCCO FORTE AUGUSTINE HOTEL

PRAGUE, CZECH REPUBLIC
COORDINATES: Ⓝ 50° 5' 20.67" Ⓔ 14° 24' 24.5916"

It seems an unusual juxtaposition: an elegant boutique hotel that houses a working monastery, but the Rocco Forte Augustine Hotel Prague makes this unique union work. Where else can you experience a private guided tour by monks through a monastery and chapel, connected to a hotel? Don't pass up this exceptional opportunity. Tucked away in a peaceful area of Prague's Lesser Town, the hotel is housed in a complex of seven interconnected buildings, dated between the 13th and 16th centuries. Immersed in the history of this fascinating city, you couldn't be anywhere else in the world.

After a day pounding Prague's cobbled streets and sightseeing, head straight to the Augustine Spa and indulge in the aptly named Step into Heaven foot massage or a relaxing St Thomas beer signature body treatment (apparently there are nourishing qualities to beer). Continuing the beer theme, start your evening with a drink in one of the hotel's two distinctive bars. The 17th-century St Thomas Brewery Bar is housed in the original cellars where the monks used to brew their own beer. Try the St Thomas beer and you'll never drink a mass-produced alternative again. Or enjoy one of the signature Angel's cocktails in the 18th-century Lichfield Cafe & Bar, located in a beautiful barrel-vaulted hall, complete with its own ceiling fresco where the Augustinian monks' refectory used to be.

Combine these unique experiences with an ambiance of warmth, impeccable service and charming staff, and you can't fail to enjoy your stay at this incredible hotel.

ICEHOTEL

JUKKASJARVI, SWEDEN
COORDINATES: (N) 67° 51' 3.0096" (E) 20° 35' 39.9156"

This winter season sees the 22nd ICEHOTEL make its dramatic appearance in the small village of Jukkasjärvi, northern Sweden. For the uninitiated, ICEHOTEL is the world's first hotel rebuilt every year, since 1990, entirely from fresh snow and ice. The 21-year journey has been something of a transformation as the hotel started out as an igloo, barely 60 square metres in size, and has now become the world's largest ice building at about 5,500 square metres.

ICEHOTEL is far more than a clever concept though. It's a life-changing experience; an ephemeral art project that has guests discovering stunning ice art and witnessing extraordinary natural phenomena. And each year is different. Founded on natural ice, harvested from the Torne River, ICEHOTEL is a leading producer of ice events around the world, namely the mother of all ICEBARs, which is a rapidly growing global franchise in its own right.

This is a pilgrimage you must make. Two hundred kilometres from the Arctic Circle, you'll catch the Northern Lights, and where else can you dance on a floor of snow and drink champagne from an ice glass? The fact that guests return year after year is testament to ICEHOTEL's natural spectacle, but also to the warm and friendly staff on hand 24 hours a day. You'll almost forget that – baby, it's cold outside.

Above
The Art Deco Suite is the work of two inspired Polish designers

Top right
The Royal Deluxe Suite is frozen luxury by Dutch artists

Bottom right
Bubblesuite is a playful interpretation of giant soap bubbles

Top left
Large Room: modern space for sleeping, working and relaxing

Bottom left
Asiatiska: historical finesse combined with techno chic

Above
Live music makes Asiatiska the place to be in Stockholm

BERNS

STOCKHOLM, SWEDEN
COORDINATES: Ⓝ 59° 19' 56.2332" Ⓔ 18° 4' 24.153"

As soon as you walk through the entrance, you'll notice the lobby is more than just a reception area, it's also a living art gallery where international and local artists display their work. Right away you'll know that the Berns Hotel is unlike any other. You won't be surprised to learn that Berns hosts the prominent Mercedes-Benz Fashion Week twice a year and is involved in projects such as Stockholm Design Week. Situated in the heart of Stockholm's business area, it only takes one phone call to the concierge to find an exclusive "in" at the hottest nightclubs and restaurants. You don't have to look far to find such places though as the Berns Hotel has its own unique restaurant, serving a modern interpretation of Asian cuisine with delectably distinctive flavours that combine favourite cuisines such as Chinese, Japanese, Thai, Vietnamese, Korean and Indian. A hotspot for both the young and the young-at-heart, the Berns Hotel also hosts its own nightclub. With live music and some of the world's coolest DJs, it's no surprise that Berns nightlife is a magnet for guests and locals alike.

But perhaps the best of Berns – and the reason guests come back time after time – is the talented and dedicated staff who treat you to the finest personal service. Guaranteed an experience rich with such delight, you'll be contemplating your next visit as you reluctantly check out.

GSTAAD PALACE

GSTAAD, SWITZERLAND
COORDINATES: Ⓝ 46° 28' 23.2962" Ⓔ 7° 17' 23.0058"

Think of a luxury hotel steeped in history, nestled in the Swiss hills overlooking Gstaad. You picture a postcard setting and the kind of jaw-dropping James Bond-style glamour that would attract the likes of Sophia Loren and Roger Moore. It's easy to see why they – and a discerning international clientele – would choose this destination and Gstaad Palace as their retreat. The natural surroundings are stunning and the stand-out hotel, with its plush interiors and refined hospitality, make you feel perfectly at home.

The Scherz family have run this fabulous hotel for three generations and their dedication is palpable throughout. The staff are known for being exceptionally warm and discreet, and will proudly take care of your every need. The 104 rooms, including various suites, are tastefully appointed and include the most luxurious three-bedroom Penthouse Suite ever built in an Alpine resort.
The hotel's five restaurants offer the best of Swiss cuisine with savoury grills, mouth-watering cheese fondues as well as Italian menus and gourmet dishes.

The activities on offer are suitably sexy and sophisticated – golf lessons, hot-air balloon rides, heli-skiing – and there's a spacious spa and health club for those in need of rest and rejuvenation. Guests can enjoy treatment rooms, saunas, steam baths, Jacuzzis, Pilates sessions, a private spa suite and relaxation rooms that enjoy commanding views. For those seeking privacy, a charming rustic hut is available above Gsteig for that extra touch of Alpine romance.
If Gstaad Palace is good enough for the world's elite, it's good enough for us.

Above
The floatation pool is part of the unique and relaxing Hammam spa experience

Top right
The Walig Hut is a simple alpine retreat high in the mountains above Gstaad

Bottom right
The Palace Spa includes a lounge, treatment rooms, saunas, steam baths and gym

Top left
Spa Suites offer comfort while indulging in treatments and therapies

Bottom left
The Penthouse Suite bedroom boasts modern luxury with a view

Above
Exclusive Spa Lofts blend indulgence and wellbeing in Swiss style

GRAND RESORT BAD RAGAZ

BAD RAGAZ, SWITZERLAND
COORDINATES: Ⓝ 47° 0' 2.8794" Ⓔ 9° 30' 14.2446"

A stay at the Grand Resort Bad Ragaz, a peaceful retreat in the Swiss mountains, is all about feeling good – focusing on regeneration and revitalisation, relaxation and contemplation. It sounds cliched but, immersed in such awe-inspiring scenery, you can't help but breathe in the fresh mountain air and feel calmed. The impressive spa facilities will assist with your feel-good mission and there's a plethora of pampering available, from massages and facials to shiatsu and reflexology, as well as a team of specialists on hand to offer specific health and wellness advice. Even the area's thermal spa water boasts beneficial properties.

But it's not all about denial and dieting, and being spa-bound. There are eight restaurants, each offering delicious gourmet cuisine. And, to get your heart pumping, there are plenty of outdoor activities, from hiking to mountain-biking, horse-riding and two championship golf courses. So expect to leave feeling like a new you.

A bird's eye view of Grand Resort Bad Ragaz in the St Gallen Rhine Valley

The Piscina dei Fiori (Flowers Pool) is the perfect place to relax and let time go by

Above
The hotel is an authentic
Art Nouveau palace with five-
star amenities

Top right
Deluxe Lake View Rooms
have balconies and occupy
corner positions

Bottom right
T Pizza, pictured at night,
is a distinctive eating place
by the pool

GRAND HOTEL TREMEZZO

LAKE COMO, ITALY
COORDINATES: Ⓝ 45° 59' 5.0598" Ⓔ 9° 13' 42.8874"

Most striking among the natural wonders of the Lake Como region are the endless and inimitable views. If you're looking to steal away with your loved one, stop looking because Grand Hotel Tremezzo is it. With unobstructed views over the sparkling waters, book a Rooftop Suite. The rooms are elegant and wonderfully spacious with panoramic terraces and Lake Como's only outdoor Jacuzzis – you'll feel like royalty.

The staff are the underlying strength of this wonderful establishment. They are utterly welcoming, and will remember your name, your room number and make conversation every time they see you.

If Italy is renowned for its stunning landscapes, it's also known for its universally loved cuisine. Be sure to reserve a table at La Terrazza to sample the menu courtesy of Gualtiero Marchesi, one of Italy's most influential gourmet chefs. There is nothing to beat breakfast on the terrace overlooking Lake Como. For relaxation there are two sumptuous pools – one floating on the lake – for lounging around and, if the surroundings need any further assistance in lulling you into a sense of luxurious oblivion, there's the T Spa with indoor heated swimming pool – perfect for a swim overlooking the lake – Jacuzzis and exceptional pampering treatments.

The outcome is one of total peace and all this is only a stone's throw away from the wonders of the legendary Villa Carlotta next door and the little villages beyond in the hills. The perfect romantic getaway with all the glamour of a James Bond film and twice the class.

ITALY

Top left
Imàgo is the Hassler's Michelin-starred restaurant with panoramic views

Bottom left
Deluxe Double Rooms combine classical charm with modern convenience

Above
The Terrace offers a rooftop perspective on Rome's historic treasures

HASSLER ROMA

ROME, ITALY
COORDINATES: Ⓝ 41° 54' 21.4266" Ⓔ 12° 29' 1.212"

In the heart of the Eternal City's historical area, the legendary five-star Hotel Hassler is minutes from many of Rome's ancient and modern landmarks. Take full advantage of the hotel's location at the top of the Spanish Steps as it's the perfect starting point for discovering St Peter's Basilica, the Coliseum, the Villa Borghese gardens and the Trevi Fountain. One of the most romantic dining experiences on record would have to be at the Michelin-starred Imago restaurant where diners can enjoy staggering picture-postcard views from the floor-to-ceiling windows while they sample delicious Italian speciality dishes. These panoramic views from the Penthouse Suite terrace sweep across the whole of Rome – the ultimate hotel destination for intimate soirees on the balcony, with attentive and discreet service. Pure understated class.

THE ST. REGIS ROME

ROME, ITALY
COORDINATES: Ⓝ 41° 54' 14.1264" Ⓔ 12° 29' 41.4816"

If you want a luxurious hotel stay in a fabulous neighbourhood in Rome, the St. Regis is for you.

Located within walking distance of local stations, as well as the Spanish Steps, Trevi Fountain and Via Veneto, the hotel actually lies in an oasis of peace. The surroundings exude luxury with stunning Renaissance interiors throughout the 161 guest rooms and suites.

The decor is matched by the service which is second-to-none. The St. Regis is the only hotel in Rome to offer an exclusive bespoke butler service with round-the-clock, discreet attention that's so good you'll never want to leave. After relaxing in the exclusive Kami Spa, the theme of excellence continues in the remarkable Vivendo restaurant – worthy of the Wall Street Journal's praise as a "bible of gastronomy" – and the di Vino wine cellar, both offering delicious Italian specialties. End the day in Le Grand Bar to complete the St. Regis experience.

Above
Step out of the St. Regis to discover the best of the Eternal City on your doorstep

Top right
The hotel's Lobby is sumptuously luxurious with an opulent interior to welcome guests

Bottom right
Deluxe Guest Rooms are embellished with architectural detail including stucco and Italian marble

42
43
44
45
46

47
48
49
50
51
52
53
54

ITALY

Top left
The Getty Suite was J.P. Getty's private wing when he lived at the aristocratic villa

Bottom left
Swimmers can choose between the heated pool or the hotel's private beach

Above
The Michelin-star Cesar Restaurant offers regional cuisine and elegant dining

LA POSTA VECCHIA HOTEL

PALO LAZIALE, ITALY
COORDINATES: Ⓝ 41° 55' 58.0398" Ⓔ 12° 6' 15.9408"

Imagine cradling a wine glass in your hand as you take in the spectacular sea view from the terrace. The sun is beginning to set and it's almost time for dinner. Instead of dining in the hotel's Michelin-star restaurant, The Cesar, tonight you have reservations for a private dinner. Instead of a table in the garden gazebo, you've chosen to

Once the summer residence of Roman emperors, this 17th-century villa is now an exclusive resort. The guest rooms reflect the hotel's sense of timeless elegance, combining antique furniture with contemporary amenities. Swim in the indoor pool overlooking the sea or head to the private beach; cycle along the coastal

SAVOIA EXCELSIOR PALACE

TRIESTE, ITALY
COORDINATES: (N) 45° 38' 59.049" (E) 13° 45' 56.556"

The Savoia Excelsior Palace simply exudes splendour. Proudly overlooking the glittering Adriatic, it is undoubtedly the finest place to stay in Trieste.

Fresh from extensive renovation, the hotel once more feels like a majestic palace and you'll certainly feel like royalty staying there. Its striking facade is adorned with classical sculptures, columns and stained glass windows. The hotel's interior design blends contemporary Italian style with the building's original classical features, bringing 1920s glamour to the present day. It's impossible to descend the impressive main staircase without feeling like a VIP.

This opulence continues into the hotel's 142 spacious rooms. All feature heavenly Starbeds layered with feathery goose down and fine linen that adapt perfectly to your body's weight. Marble bathrooms with enormous bathtubs, fluffy bathrobes and luscious toiletries will make you feel completely pampered. The views of the bay from your private balcony are unsurpassable, especially those overlooking the magnificent Castello di Miramare on the waterfront.

Dining at the Savoia is really something to write home about. Start your day by enjoying an ample continental breakfast while looking out over impossibly clear waters. Come evening, delightfully fresh seafood awaits you at the Savoy Restaurant – the baked sea bass with porcini mushrooms is exquisite. Savouring a Trieste Pink Cocktail, the Savoia's signature drink, under the elegant shell-shaped ceiling in Le Rive Bar is certainly the best way to soak up the atmosphere of this elegant hotel.

Above
Completely refurbished, the Savoia Excelsior Palace retains grand hotel charm

Top right
Superior Rooms are spacious, comfortable and have beautiful sea views

Bottom right
Breakfast overlooking the Gulf of Trieste: room service is available 24 hours a day

ITALY

Top left
Bedroom of the Ambassador Suite with sea views and private terrace

Bottom left
The Terrazza Tiberio Restaurant serves mouthwatering Italian food and fine wine

Above
The Bellevue Royal Suite is modern chic with a rooftop sun deck

CAPRI TIBERIO PALACE HOTEL & SPA

ISLAND OF CAPRI, ITALY
COORDINATES: Ⓝ 40° 33' 3.3084" Ⓔ 14° 14' 49.3512"

The Capri Tiberio Palace is a sight for sore eyes. Perched above the village, this renovated hotel is privately owned by an Italian family and captures the spirit of Capri – arguably one of the most stylish places in the world. Carefully balanced powder blues, lemon golds and coral reds throughout lend a sense of peace and contemporary freshness.
The 40 rooms and 20 suites enjoy breathtaking sea-facing balconies and sun-filled terraces respectively. The Terrazza Tiberio restaurant serves exquisite dishes bursting with sunny flavour – try the Amberjack Tartare with cherry tomatoes, olives from Gaeta and caper flowers ice cream or the mouthwatering ravioli Capres, leaving room for the delectable bourbon vanilla and Venezuelan chocolate mousse. Indoor and outdoor pools, a fitness centre and the gorgeous Spa Tiberio will put paid to any lingering stress, and the Jacky Bar breathes 1960's Cuban chic for a nightcap at the end of the day. The finest hotel to get away from it all.

CAESAR AUGUSTUS

ISLAND OF CAPRI, ITALY
COORDINATES: (N) 40° 33' 29.8908" (E) 14° 13' 25.0602"

From its spectacular and majestic clifftop position, Hotel Caesar Augustus commands respect and elicits gasps of admiration. The family-owned hotel has for three generations welcomed guests to the village of Anacapri in an exceptionally luxurious setting.

Far from the madding crowd, the decor pays homage to the building's historical background – a Russian prince laid claim to the cliff at the beginning of the 1900's – and to its geographical situation perched above the Bay of Naples. Overlooking Mount Vesuvius, Sorrento and Ischia, the views are jaw-droppingly beautiful, and are echoed throughout the hotel in each and every detail and aspect of the service provided.

The emphasis is on relaxation, intimacy and feeling special. The chef is known to make an appearance around the pool offering freshly picked and cooked treats straight from his herb garden. It has been said that you'll never eat fresher tomato and basil salad this side of Naples.

The property is peppered with secluded "cuddle spots" and secret gardens. Thoughts turn to romance as the sun goes down, and the hotel and gardens transform into a magical wonderland bathed in candlelight and the soothing sounds of piano music coming from the lobby. At this point you'll want to stop off for a nightcap at the bar, maybe enjoy an excellent cigar and contemplate the lights twinkling across the horizon. As you return to your room to find it scented with lavender and your bed freshly turned down, your thoughts turn to tomorrow and the prospect of another sun-filled day in paradise.

Above
A bath with a view: 1,000 feet above the sea and sights of Capri

Top right
The panoramic swimming pool is the most spectacular on the island

Bottom right
At night, gentle candlelight fills the hotel's elegant dining room

Top left
Superior Rooms are elegantly Italian and warmly modern

Bottom left
The hotel interior is a blend of fresh and vibrant colours

Above
Splendid Venice is just steps away from St Mark's Square

SPLENDID VENICE

VENICE, ITALY
COORDINATES: Ⓝ 36° 59' 31.725" Ⓔ 27° 20' 14.841"

Arguably one of the most beautiful cities in the world, Venice is an intricate maze of weaving canals and floating palazzi. There are many nooks and crannies to this city, but few would fail to recognise Piazza San Marco and its surrounding archways. Visitors flock here for a taste of the past preserved. Lovers come to absorb the centuries of romance and art that are Venice's very lifeblood. Splendid Venice, a luxury hotel just steps away from Rialto Bridge,

peace, sheltered by canals on either side and away from the city hubbub. This ancient palace houses elegant rooms and suites dressed in traditional Venetian style with a modern touch. Overlooking a beautiful courtyard is Le Maschere, one of Venice's most acclaimed restaurants which attracts the locals in their droves – always a good sign. Set in a relaxed atmosphere, it's ideal for discovering Venetian cuisine, a distinctive wine list, and enjoying the intimacy of the hotel

After dinner, take a pew at Splendid Venice's bar for one of their famous Bellinis or, even better, try the barman's own creations. Sit back and watch the world and its gondolas glide past. We recommend you contact Les Clefs D'Or concierge service at the hotel before you arrive to make your stay as romantic as possible. Water taxis, tickets to the opera or a museum, car rental, restaurant reservations, baby-sitting – nothing is too much trouble.

L'ALBERETA

ERBUSCO, ITALY
COORDINATES: Ⓝ 45° 36' 29.6598" Ⓔ 9° 58' 48.3312"

Escaping to the lush hills of Franciacorta and the luxurious L'Albereta Hotel is just what you need to leave all your troubles well behind you. Whatever you do, do not miss the opportunity to thoroughly pamper yourself at the highly acclaimed Henri Chenot Spa. There's a selection of seven different treatments designed to cater specifically to your needs and recapture wellbeing. Be it anti-ageing, detoxifying or reflexology – it's all a sensory treat straight from heaven. If you're fortunate to visit in September and you like your wine, take advantage of a special weekend offer that allows guests to discover the region and its traditions. L'Albereta, owned by the Moretti family, guides wine lovers through the taste labs in the family wineries of Bellavista and Contadi Castaldi. You can train your senses and learn about the wines and food from the Franciacorta area by meeting the people who actually manufacture these products. Elsewhere, The Gualtieno Marchesi Restaurant dishes up classics like Gualtiero's trademark veal fillet Rossini, as well as experimental dishes like the Andy Warhol-inspired "serial" pasta. The resort's close proximity to Lake Iseo, and the abundance of art and quirky boutiques typical to the Lombardy region, should tempt you away for the day. The countryside is spectacular and there for the exploring with its gently sloping hills where vineyards nestle and shimmer in the sun. They are Franciacorta's crowning glory and L'Albereta is the jewel in its crown.

Above
Sala Scacchi extends a warm, five-star welcome to guests

Top right
Superior Rooms feature luxurious silks and damask

Bottom right
View of the exclusive hotel from the vineyard

Top left
The pool has views of the unspoiled waters of the Tyrrhenian Sea

Bottom left
All rooms are fully equipped, air-conditioned and have wi-fi connection

Above
Il Pellicano is a cluster of villas set in perfumed Mediterranean gardens

IL PELLICANO

TUSCANY, ITALY
COORDINATES: Ⓝ 42° 22' 25.5612" Ⓔ 11° 11' 14.7084"

If you want the intimacy of your own home paired with unrivalled splendour and dedicated staff working to fulfil your individual needs and desires, then look no further than the exclusive Il Pellicano.

What started off in 1965 with just 18 guest rooms has grown to 50 rooms and suites, and six cottages spread over 17 acres. Yet the hotel has still managed to retain the effortless sophistication and special atmosphere that is its heart and soul.

Il Pellicano provides you with all the resources necessary to make your stay unforgettable. Treat yourself to a luxury massage at the Pelliclub, take a one-of-a-kind cooking course with the hotel's two Michelin-star chef, swim in the heated saltwater pool, or spend the day island hopping on one of the hotel's boats. With former guests including Charlie Chaplin and Gianni Agnelli, you're in good company.

THE ST. REGIS FLORENCE

FLORENCE, ITALY
COORDINATES: (N) 43° 46' 19.6824" (E) 11° 14' 42.381"

Prepare yourself for a sensual treat as you arrive in the legendary city of Florence, especially if The St. Regis Florence is home during your stay. The newly renovated luxury hotel is the epitome of elegance and world-class hospitality.

Overlooking the Arno River, in a sumptuous 19th-century Renaissance palace, all of Florence's rich heritage can be found under this hotel's spectacular roof. You're within walking distance of the city's wonderful attractions and right at the heart of the extraordinary atmosphere it emanates.

Within the hotel's walls there are 81 spacious guest rooms and 19 distinctive suites decorated in the Medici, Florentine and Renaissance style. The signature suite is designed by Bottega Veneta's creative director and celebrates serene, muted neutrals mixed with pieces from the brand's furniture collection. Elsewhere in the rooms and suites, guests are treated to sumptuous beds, state-of-the-art sound systems and TV, top-of-the-range finishing and elegant bathrooms. The round-the-clock St. Regis butler service completes the experience.

Italy's cuisine is showcased in the highly acclaimed restaurant Etichetta Pinchiorri that successfully combines innovative and traditional dishes with an enviable wine list. Everywhere you look, the hotel is a feast for the senses, with its fine-art ceilings dating back to the 19th century and a spectacular hand-blown Murano glass chandelier. For pure indulgence, after a day exploring the city, we recommend you book into the Iridium Suites for a relaxing or rejuvenating treatment. We suspect you'll never want to check out.

Above
Ballroom decor, featuring period frescos, pays homage to the city's artistic heritage

Top right
The Royal Suite Terrace offers a champagne view of the River Arno and Medici Florence

Bottom right
The Presidential Da Vinci Suite combines the art of hospitality and the Renaissance

Top left
Del Bosco Bedroom:
elegance and romance
with Italian style

Bottom left
Barriques cellar: Brunello
di Montalcino wine is a
long-standing tradition

Above
The Pool: serene against
a typically Tuscan backdrop

CASTIGLION DEL BOSCO

MONTALCINO, ITALY
COORDINATES: Ⓝ 43° 5' 3.1128" Ⓔ 11° 25' 19.524"

Originally an 18th-century medieval village, Castiglion del Bosco has been uniquely converted into a luxurious boutique retreat. More of a Tuscan country experience than a resort or hotel, this gourmet's dream is ideally located in the heart of the Brunello di Montalcino wine-making region. Spend your days wine tasting in the estate's private winery, exploring the flavours of Tuscan cooking in the culinary academy or even truffle hunting. Expect to dine on delicacies, such as homemade wild boar sausage and exquisite Pecorino di Pienza, as well as the estate's own honey and olive oil. After such indulgence, you may just want to lounge by the pool. But, if you feel the need to exercise, then fear not as there are plenty of activities available to help you burn off some of those calories, from golf to tennis and hiking to horse riding. Elsewhere we recommend the cocoon of the Care Suite Spa with its earthy hues and Tuscan character that reflect the refined soul of this extraordinary property.

KEMPINSKI HOTEL SAN LAWRENZ

GOZO, MALTA
COORDINATES: (N) 36° 3' 13.485" (E) 14°12' 32.0502"

Described as Malta's little sister, Gozo is a charming island that enjoys life at a slower pace than its Maltese siblings. What Gozo has in spades is natural beauty and a rich heritage.

There's also the Kempinksi Hotel San Lawrenz. This honey-coloured hotel heralds Maltese architecture, framed by vast, idyllic grounds that lie close to the harbour and the Azure Window, one of the best diving spots in the Mediterranean. It's also the only eco-certified hotel in Gozo where vegetables, fruit and herbs are sourced from its gardens, bringing extra freshness to all the menus. You must explore the pretty grounds to capture the aromas and see where the tomatoes on your plate actually came from. The service is unerringly friendly and the views exceptional in The Gazebo Garden Restaurant and the Pool Bar, which is open in the summer months. There's also the Café & Lounge with a cocktail terrace perfect for happy hour and sunset. The largest sandy beach, Ramla Bay, and the seaside resorts of Marsalforn and Xlendi, are the better known beaches, but seek out the little hidden bays and inlets that play to your illusion of being alone on the island. The hotel's Ayurveda Centre is staffed by world-class professionals extensively trained in India, offering a myriad of treatments for physical and mental wellbeing. Meanwhile, the hotel's Indian chef will dish up your dream meal. It's tempting to keep the magic of Gozo all to yourself.

Above
The hotel boasts a fabulous outdoor pool, terraces and landscaped grounds

Top right
Rooms and suites have a tranquil and soothing rustic ambience

Bottom right
The luxury spa features an indoor pool and offers relaxing treatments

Top left
All 93 Suites feature comfort, elegant interior design and private open spaces

Bottom left
Hospitality and excellence are core values at SHA: a paradise for health and wellness

Above
Healthy cuisine is based on macrobiotic principles and adapted to local style

SHA WELLNESS CLINIC

ALICANTE, SPAIN
COORDINATES: Ⓝ 38° 33' 36.5292" Ⓔ 0° 4' 26.9322"

Are you feeling stressed? Do you have problems sleeping? Would you like to lose weight, detox or slow down the inevitable ageing process? Help is waiting for you on a beautiful Spanish mountainside, overlooking the Mediterranean Sea at the luxurious SHA Wellness Clinic. Using a combination of ancient Eastern wisdom

healthy – but delicious – food in a chic environment without a rigorous programme, then you'll be equally at home. As you would expect, the SHA Spa boasts an extensive treatment and therapies list from hydrotherapy to music therapy and massages to facials. An open-air massage, accompanied by the heavenly views, is an instant calmer.

Top left
An elegant Executive Suite bedroom with views of the Andalusian coastline

Bottom left
The Spa Sunlight Pool: dedicated to relaxation, beauty and wellness

Above
The Blue Bar for Spanish tapas or classic cocktails in a luxurious setting

FINCA CORTESIN HOTEL & GOLF

CASARES, SPAIN
COORDINATES: Ⓝ 36° 23' 38.7558" Ⓦ 5° 13' 31.9974"

Lovers of golf and understated elegance, prepare to swoon. Finca Cortesin is a luxury hotel, golf, spa and villa resort between Sotogrande and Marbella that will take your breath away.

Lying in 530 acres of rolling landscape, the original finca is a traditional farmhouse surrounded by beautifully assimilated new buildings. There are 67 guest suites with sweeping views of the ocean and an 18-hole golf course, which is home of the prestigious Jack Nicklaus Academy and Volvo World Match Play Championship.

There are three restaurants – Schilo, El Jardin de Victor and Don Giovanni – and a friendly hotel bar where you can personalise your cocktails. Two poolside bars serve delicious lunches, and there's a spa and exclusive boutique area to complete the relaxed experience. The new Beach Club is causing ripples among guests with its elegant gardens, teak-decked sun-lounging space and beautiful infinity pool. Enjoy a leisurely Mediterranean lunch and soak up the serene atmosphere.

The outdoor pool is punctuated by tropical palm trees

56
57
58
59
60
61

Top left
Terraced pools cascade
down the hillside

Bottom left
The Eden Room has a
private pool and garden

Above
The Amphitheatre with
a spectacular backdrop

HOTEL HACIENDA NA XAMENA

IBIZA, SPAIN
COORDINATES: Ⓝ 39° 4' 44.7558" Ⓔ 1° 25' 13.1442"

The views from Hotel Hacienda Na Xamena are just breathtaking. Perched atop white cliffs on the quieter north-east side of the island, the hotel is a haven for the more discerning Ibiza crowd. The hotel's rooms are quirkily built into the surrounding cliffs, angled towards the bay and Mediterranean. Incidentally, this panorama is replicated from the comfort of your own in-room Jacuzzi.

The sensory indulgence continues in the spa with the Thalassotherapy saltwater spa treatment, developed exclusively for the hotel. Set in the heated saltwater cascade pools overlooking the sea, a series of therapeutic jets reinvigorate stressed and strained bodies. For an additional wow-factor, book your session to coincide with Ibiza's spectacular sunset. With three terraced gourmet restaurants, culinary classes with the head chef, exclusive boat excursions and unforgettable mountain hikes, you'll never want to leave Hotel Hacienda Na Xamena – "the Soul of Ibiza."

Hotel Hacienda, perched high above the Mediterranean in an unspoilt pine wood, enjoys fabulous views

Each Executive Suite features a private pool

Above
The Kymata Restaurant serves
light à la carte lunches

Top right
Private access to the sandy
beach and shady Cabanas

Bottom right
Each Executive Suite offers
luxurious accommodation
and a private pool

CONSTANTINOU BROS ASIMINA SUITES HOTEL

PAPHOS, CYPRUS
COORDINATES: Ⓝ 34° 44' 38.1156" Ⓔ 32° 25' 47.4738"

If you're looking for rest and relaxation in serene beachfront surroundings, then Asimina Suites Hotel ticks all the boxes. It's an adults-only hotel – unique in Paphos – so there's no chance of the peace and tranquillity being shattered by over-excited children.

From the moment you arrive, when you're ushered into a private check-in lounge and welcomed with cold towels, drinks and canapes, you'll feel like a VIP. While relaxing on your padded – yes padded – sun lounger by you can expect refreshing cold towels and complimentary fresh fruit to appear just as you're feeling warm or peckish. At the raise of a hand, a friendly, smiling staff member will be at your side with the drinks menu. Throughout your stay nothing is too much trouble, but there's no constant harassment from over-zealous staff. Add to this grown-up ambience the fact that there are no big crowds – the hotel only has 121 suites – no pre-breakfast rush for sun beds – there's Elixir spa, and now you're talking holiday. The suites are luxuriously appointed with spacious marble bathrooms. Treat yourself and book one of the seafront Executive Suites which boast their own private pool and Jacuzzi as well as a private beach cabana. You're spoilt for choice when it comes to dining, with four restaurants and two bars, but if you need to impress a loved one, then you can't beat a romantic dinner as the sun sets at the Kymata beachfront restaurant.

The hotel's infinity pool
looks out onto a magnificent
Mediterranean seascape

Above
The hotel's private
sandy beach is located
in a secluded bay

Top right
Asian and Italian dishes,
as well as fresh fish, are
served in a modern setting

Bottom right
Luxury accommodation
with a private pool
and expansive sea view

DAIOS COVE LUXURY RESORTS & VILLAS

CRETE, GREECE
COORDINATES: Ⓝ 35° 7' 33.4632" Ⓔ 25° 45' 9.4464"

Set on a hillside overlooking its own secluded beach, Daios Cove is the ultimate getaway. Lying on the northern coast of the island of Crete, just minutes from the town of Aghios Nikolaos, this stunning resort dazzles from every angle with its sublime views. The interior and exterior design blend minimalist, modern and sumptuous, as the architecture integrates seamlessly into its natural environment.

There are 39 villas and 261 rooms with priceless sea views. Luxuriously appointed, light and airy, they afford large living spaces and flawless style,

with many of the luxury suites and villas including a private seawater swimming pool.

The exclusive ambience is complemented by impeccable round-the-clock service and exquisite dining. Villa guests should take advantage of the Cove Club, which provides exclusive service with the utmost discretion and professionalism. Breakfast sets the scene for a perfect stay in your room, as you're greeted by blue skies, views of the shimmering Mediterranean and a healthy selection of delicious options to suit every

palate. Food lovers are in for a treat as there are top-class restaurants and bars, including two à la carte and a beach bar – Ocean for creative and fine Italian cuisine and Taverna for the best of contemporary Greek and Cretan cuisine.

Daios Cove takes relaxation and pampering very seriously, and consequently the fabulous spa is second-to-none. For total wellbeing, there's a state-of-the-art fitness centre with two indoor pools, and the water sports and diving centre are ideal for enjoying the fabulous coastal location.

GREECE

64
65
66

67
68

Top left
The Royal Grande Suite has private outdoor and indoor pools

Bottom left
The living area of the Royal Grande Suite is on three levels

Above
The Six Senses Spa offers a range of signature treatments

ELOUNDA PENINSULA ALL SUITE HOTEL

CRETE, GREECE
COORDINATES: Ⓝ 35° 14' 27.7872" Ⓔ 25° 44' 0.2502"

If you're looking for an intimate beachfront hotel and a relaxing holiday with your loved one, then Elounda Peninsula All Suites Hotel is ideal. Think spacious suites with private pools, romantic dining, a tranquil beach with waiter service and luxury yachts waiting to whisk you away to an isolated cove for the day.

It may sound like a contradiction, but if you're holidaying as a family and need activities to keep everyone entertained, then this hotel works for you too. Your children are entertained in the kids' club or with swimming or tennis lessons, while you relax in the award-winning Six Senses Spa or out on the golf course.

All this is combined with genuinely friendly staff and breathtaking views across the sea, while you sip cocktails at Serenes' Bar. The privacy of the suites means the Elounda Peninsula has become the ultimate hideaway for A-list celebrities everywhere, making the area the luxury destination in Greece.

HOTEL GRANDE BRETAGNE
A LUXURY COLLECTION HOTEL

ATHENS, GREECE
COORDINATES: Ⓝ 37° 58' 34.356" Ⓔ 23° 44' 7.3566"

With breathtaking views of the famed Acropolis and Parthenon, regal Constitution Square and the Parliament, lush Lycabettus Hill and the original Olympic Stadium, the multi-awarded five-star Hotel Grande Bretagne offers an unrivalled perspective of Athens' mythical history. Located opposite Syntagma Square, and within walking distance of exclusive shopping areas and museums, the hotel enjoys an ideal location in the city centre. This eight-storey, 19th-century building exudes wealth and refinement from the first impression, and won the 2011 Green Key, Condé Nast Traveler and Travel + Leisure award.

The beauty of this hotel is many-fold, but the very foundations of its appeal lie in the seamless blend of old-world elegance with eye-catching modernity, all placed with an utter sense of refinement and great taste. Book one of the elegant suites and enjoy personalised butler service, as well as plush fabrics, original artwork and an outstanding collection of antiques. In edition to in-room dining, an experience not to be missed is a meal at the GB Roof Garden Restaurant where a sensational view of the Acropolis is the perfect backdrop for such a culinary experience. We recommend, for example, the roasted shrimp teriyaki or the white grouper fillet – both outstanding dishes. While you're up on the roof, perhaps before your luxury dining experience, take a dip in the rooftop swimming pool and let the views of an illuminated Athens and the magic of this timeless city wash over you.

Above
GB Roof Garden restaurant and bar with views of the Acropolis

Top right
The rooftop pool and bar are a refreshing retreat for total relaxation

Bottom right
Grand Suites feature warm elegance in living areas and a secluded bedroom

GREECE

Top left
The shipwreck at Zakynthos is a local attraction

Bottom left
Royal Spa Villa has its own small private estate

Above
Villas enjoy breathtaking views of the Ionian Sea

PORTO ZANTE VILLAS

ZAKYNTHOS, GREECE
COORDINATES: Ⓝ 37° 50' 21.879" Ⓔ 20° 51' 45.3888"

The island of Zakynthos, once named the Flower of the East, is the perfect setting for the exclusive Porto Zante Villas. Settled along a spotless beach, with breathtaking views of the Ionian Sea, the villas provide complete peace and privacy for those wanting to escape from it all.

Individual gardens and private pools mean that you need never leave your villa, but if you ever feel adventurous, the gorgeous private beach awaits you. The villas offer magnificent open living areas, with striking glass doors opening onto private terraces. The warm Greek sun bathes the bedrooms in golden light and the antique marble-lined bathrooms invite you to indulge your inner Greek god. Fluffy Armani Casa bathrobes and lavish Bulgari toiletries – there for the taking – complete this picture of utter luxury.

Zakynthos is a real treasure island for children. Guided excursions to the nearby village, days of splashing fun at the water park and a mini golf course promise to keep your children entertained for hours. It's the perfect opportunity for you to experience the resort's in-villa spa treatments, where a variety of ancient Greek techniques and the relaxing powers of aromatherapy will inspire wellbeing in the tensest of bodies.

Eating at the Club House Restaurant is a must. What could be more enjoyable than sampling deliciously fresh Greek and Mediterranean cuisine while looking out over impossibly blue water towards the beautiful neighbouring island of Kefalonia? Alternatively, the in-villa dining service is a romantic way to enjoy the total tranquillity of this enchanting island.

MUSEUM HOTEL

CAPPADOCIA, TURKEY
COORDINATES: (N) 38° 37' 44.364" (E) 34° 48' 21.009"

The Museum Hotel is more than its name suggests. Arriving at this unique and distinctive hotel in Cappadocia is like stepping into another world filled with natural, vibrant splendour and steeped in history, which has witnessed the glories of Greek, Byzantine and Ottoman cultures. Views of the Red Valley must count among the most breathtaking in the world and the hotel setting itself is just as extraordinary. The hotel, which sits upon ruins and enjoys lush gardens, is carved out of sandstone. What were once caves have been transformed into a magical wonderland. Rooms vary in size and layout, and each has its own distinct character. The decor and detail include exquisite antique furniture, luxurious comforts – who would have thought you could ever have free wi-fi in your own cave? – a personal Jacuzzi with staggering views of the valleys and Mount Erciyes, spacious marble showers, cosy fireplaces as well as personal wellness services. Elsewhere an infinity-like pool invites guests to bask in its beauty and the Lil'a restaurant offers top-quality regional cuisine.

It's the staff here that make all the difference. Their approach to every aspect of service is professional, friendly and extremely attentive. Rest assured that your every wish will be attended to. Among the experiences that are not to be missed is the exhilarating hot-air balloon ride over the valley.

If you dream of escaping the stresses of modern life and stepping back in time to a world of historical charm, this unique boutique hotel should be at the top of your wish list of world-class destinations.

Above
The Sultan Cave bedroom is one of 30 rooms and suites which have been carefully restored

Top right
The Guvercinlik (Dovecote) Cave is carved from sandstone and offers modern amenities

Bottom right
The spectacular infinity swimming pool cascades into the historic hotel grounds

Top left
International cuisine
in a cosy atmosphere

Bottom left
Sleek luxury in the centre
of Turkey's historic city

Above
Istanbul's premier
contemporary boutique hotel

THE SOFA HOTEL

ISTANBUL, TURKEY
COORDINATES: Ⓝ 41° 3' 1.7136" Ⓔ 28° 59' 33.6438"

Amid the hustle and bustle of Istanbul's trendy Nisantasi neighbourhood is a haven of peace called The Sofa Hotel. This luxury boutique hotel serves as a stylish pied-a-terre for visitors to the gateway linking Europe to Asia. Though the onus is on design, with works of art on display and contemporary finishing, there's substance under the surface as well as style. Serenity and comfort are the key words here with attentive and discreet concierge service, personal touches in your room, such as a complimentary bottle of water, chocolates, luxury toiletries, high technology and a wet room shower. There are 82 guest rooms, including 17 Executive Suites which we highly recommend as a luxurious home from home. The Cafe Sofa serves up delicious world cuisine, and the SANITAS SPA will get you back in shape in no time for your shopping and sightseeing trips – Turkish baths, anti-ageing and thalassotherapy should soothe away the stress.

A'JIA HOTEL

ISTANBUL, TURKEY
COORDINATES: (N) 41° 6' 7.7826" (E) 29° 3' 58.3884"

Set on the Asian banks of the Bosphorus, the best way to arrive at A'Jia Hotel has to be in Bond-style glamour via the hotel's speedboat (Bond girl not provided). This traditional Ottoman-style mansion is an intimate boutique hotel boasting 16 contemporary rooms – think polished wooden floors and white linen. It's well worth upgrading to one of the top-floor suites that have their own private balconies with stunning Bosphorus views.

Spend your days exploring the bustling vibrancy of Istanbul before heading back to this haven of calm and enjoy dinner à deux at the waterfront restaurant (don't miss the fantastic mushroom risotto and souffle). If you're looking for a hotel with endless facilities then there are plenty of larger options to choose from in Istanbul; the emphasis at A'Jia Hotel is personalised service – and it's simply the perfect romantic weekend escape.

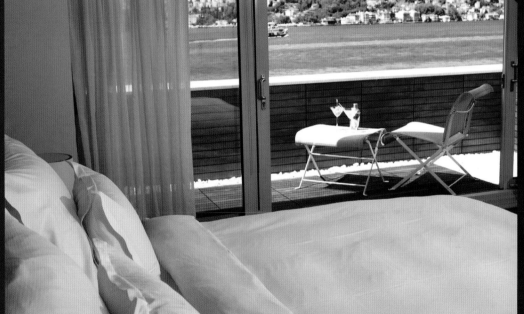

Above
The sun deck has dramatic views of the Bosphorus

Top right
Rooms with private balconies offer modern style and luxury

Bottom right
This boutique hotel is a traditional Ottoman mansion

TURKEY

69
70
71
72

Top left
Rooms have a balcony
or terrace overlooking
the Aegean Sea

Bottom left
The Chill Out Lounge
is a place to slow down
and relax

Above
The Six Senses Spa
offers rejuvenation,
beauty and fitness

KEMPINSKI HOTEL BARBAROS BAY BODRUM

BODRUM, TURKEY
COORDINATES: Ⓝ 36° 59' 31.725" Ⓔ 27° 30' 36.162"

Bodrum has endured a turbulent past, making it the ideal destination for history buffs. But for those more familiar with Alexander McQueen than Alexander the Great, who captured the city in 334 BC, the Kempinski Hotel is the place to experience Bodrum's more stylish side. Gliding through the Aegean Sea aboard a luxury yacht to the Kempinski's private marina is the finest way to check in. All the hotel's magnificent rooms have a private balcony or terrace which commands breathtaking views of the private bay below. Book to stay in a Presidential Suite and greet the morning from your alfresco whirlpool on the terrace.

To discover the countless secret coves around the Bodrum peninsula, hire a gulet, a traditional Turkish fishing boat. Spend the morning swimming and fishing, and be back in time for breakfast, conveniently served until 12 noon. Kempinski breakfasts are not to be missed – a selection of traditional fare and rich Turkish coffee. Kids love the Turtle Club Restaurant where they can eat fun food and make new friends. Of course, there are traditional hammam treatments in the Six Senses Spa for a taste of authentic relaxation, as well as excellent dining options at one of the hotel's restaurants. Something for the memory bank – dangling your toes in the sea as you eat the catch of the day at the Barbarossa Restaurant beachside, before retiring to the cool Barblue for a nightcap at the end of a perfect day.

ARARAT PARK HYATT MOSCOW

MOSCOW, RUSSIA
COORDINATES: N 55° 45' 36.2376" E 37° 37' 17.4066

Relaxing in contemporary surroundings, vodka on the rocks in hand, sampling Beluga black caviar (naturally), it's hard to believe that you're in central Moscow, albeit ten storeys above the city in a stunning hotel rooftop bar. However, there's no need to pinch yourself, the vista you're taking in is definitely The Kremlin and famous Bolshoi Theatre.

The Ararat Park Hyatt Moscow boasts an unbeatable location, just minutes from these iconic Russian buildings and Red Square, as well as various restaurants and stylish shops.

Traditional and elegant, but not old-fashioned and stuffy, the architecture and design of the hotel also combine modern elements.

You're made to feel special as soon as you walk through the door. Nothing is too much trouble, whether it's a coffee at 4am, explaining the menu in the unique Armenian restaurant or suggestions for dining out.

And all delivered with a smile, in eloquent English. Quite a coup in a city that is still fairly new to mass tourism and coming to grips with service levels that we now expect globally.

The cosmopolitan yet cozy design of the guest rooms and suites simply adds to this welcoming ambiance. After a busy day exploring, refresh in the indoor swimming pool – one of the hotel's best-kept secrets – or indulge in a spa treatment. And if you don't fancy venturing back out for dinner, then there's something for everyone in the hotel's three restaurants.

Any stereotypical preconceptions you may have of Moscow as a dated and inhospitable destination will be blown away when you stay here.

Above
The Conservatory Terrace overlooks Moscow's famous Red Square

Top right
Cafe Ararat features authentic Armenian cuisine in tasteful surroundings

Bottom right
The Quantum Health Club offers spa treatments and a relaxing pool

One of two pools in the
Grand SPA Rodina complex

Above
Black Magnolia restaurant serves fine Mediterranean cuisine

Top right
The hotel Library is in the style of Stalinist neoclassicism

Bottom right
Sophisticated design and comfort combine with functionality

RODINA GRAND
HOTEL & SPA

Rodina Grand Hotel & Spa is elegantly poised on the hill overlooking the town of Sochi. Steeped in history, this jewel in the crown of the Russian Riviera has home. Staff make you feel welcome and the calming effect of this serene location is impossible to resist. Given the high-powered and well-heeled are just 40 finely appointed rooms, including the Junior and Deluxe Suites with lavish views of the gardens or sea. Whatever you do make sure you

Top left
Bliss St Petersburg offers signature spa treatments within the hotel

Bottom left
The modern chic of the hotel's Wonderful Rooms reflects all-hours energy

Above
miX in St Petersburg serves up a stylish blend of cuisine and culture

decor with elegant tradition to create the epitome of funky boutique chic. The WOW suite is perfect for escaping the bustling streets of the city. The living room breathes uber-cool chic with crisp white sofas, Ortenzia gold lamps and enough cutting-edge technology to keep you busy for hours. When you finally drag yourself away from your room and fancy some exercise, get the adrenaline flowing at SWEAT. As the name suggests, this gym takes itself seriously but is never intimidating. There are elliptical machines for gentle exercise and state-of-the-art treadmills for regulars. You'll have earned a treatment at the hotel's BLISS SPA that offers a dazzling choice of treatments with facials, a luxe nail lounge, steam room and Jacuzzi – there's something to please everyone. You'll have earned a complimentary visit to the WET splash pool, perhaps with a little detour via the brownie buffet after. The miX in St Petersburg restaurant and miXup bar are great fun when the sun goes down. Alain Ducasse's restaurant is counted as the best in Russia, featuring a menu packed with some of his signature dishes, as well as fabulous Russian-inspired cuisine. If you take a seat at the chef's table in the Chandelier Room, you can even watch the food being prepared through the open kitchen. The wine cellar is eclectic and well thought-out to cater for a wide range of guests from around the world. There are more than 120 wines to choose from with the help of the team.

Don't go to bed without popping into the trendy miXup terrace or miXup bar which have magical views of St Petersburg's night skyline. You can sip on a creative cocktail and strut your stuff to the sounds of the in-house DJ until the small hours, before slinking back to your luxury pad and sinking into the plumpest, comfiest bed ever. Some reckon this hotel is the best thing since the launch of Sputnik. They might just be right.

Left
Get together, drink and dance at the Antonio Citterio-designed miXup Bar

Above
W St Petersburg is a modern wonder romanced by the city's elegance

AFRICA & INDIAN OCEAN

CONTENTS

Laze above the resort's azure
lagoon and enjoy the luxury
of an exclusive Water Villa

Above
Perched on three-metre-high stilts, Ocean View Villas have their own private infinity pool

Top right
Fashala Lounge boasts spectacular ocean views and a gourmet menu

Bottom right
Deluxe Pool Villas each have a private garden, beach front, infinity pool and sun deck

SHANGRI-LA'S VILLINGILI RESORT & SPA MALDIVES

ADDU ATOLL, MALDIVES
COORDINATES: Ⓢ 0° 40' 19.7256" Ⓔ 73° 11' 29.0214"

Shangri-La's Villingili Resort and Spa, Maldives is unique. It's the first luxury destination south of the equator on the island of Villingili, at the southern-most tip of the Addu Atoll. The resort stands out for its utmost respect for nature. Picture a scene where vegetation is so lush and plentiful, lagoons and nature trails so untouched, you'd be forgiven for thinking this beauty was man-made. And that's where you'd be wrong. The resort enjoys kilometres of coastline and sandy beach, and goes to great lengths to ensure that the seven distinct styles of villa accommodation blend organically into their environment. From private villas with an ocean view to tree-house retreats, the feel is spacious and stylish. Decked terraces, outdoor showers, free-standing bath tubs looking out to the horizon, hammocks, private pools and the ocean as your front garden – being at one with nature can't get any better than this. The staff are local, highly professional and extremely friendly. You'll be pampered, but discreetly and without pretension. Your villa host will fix you a cocktail, book you a treatment at the fabulous CHI, The Spa, recommend a dish from one of the three restaurants on site or arrange a bicycle tour of the neighbouring islands. A tour is ideal for exploring the unspoilt villages, observing everyday life and chatting to the locals over coffee. For serious glamour and escapism, why don't you set sail in a luxury yacht and have lunch on the equator? It's something very few can say they have done and it will revolutionise your idea of luxury in the Maldives.

MALDIVES

80
81
82

83
84
85
86
87
88
89
90

Top left
A romantic Dining Pavilion for an unforgettable experience

Bottom left
Most of the luxurious Villas are perched on stilts over the lagoon

Above
Restaurants serve progressive world cuisine and international specialities

TAJ EXOTICA RESORT & SPA, MALDIVES

SOUTH MALE ATOLL, MALDIVES
COORDINATES: Ⓝ 4° 6' 10.965" Ⓔ 73° 31' 31.44"

Exclusive, private and romantic island resorts don't come much better than Taj Exotica Resort & Spa in the Maldives. The luxury speedboat drops you off – Male International Airport is just 15 minutes away, though you wouldn't know it – and from thereon in it's "welcome to the slow lane". Stress makes way for sensory overload as tropical plants, clear blue lagoon and flawlessly white sand become your own back garden.

The various Villas are sumptuously designed, each as charming as the next, with palm-thatched roofing, natural wood finishing and Maldivian decor. The term, heaven on Earth, may be overused, but when there's only the deep blue sea and the sunset to block your view, we reckon heaven on Earth seals it. Only a wooden ladder separates you from a refreshing dip in the lagoon – a great spot to watch the sun rise and set.

A favourite is the fitness centre, open until the last guest leaves and located over the lagoon at the far end of the island. So work out, practise yoga or take a class, without missing that legendary sunset. The nearby Jiva Grande Spa specialises in Indian rejuvenation and aromatherapy, as well as Alepa – literally the act of anointing the body with oil – that will leave you floating like a feather. Take advantage of the butler service to fully plan your activities, and end the day with a private dining experience and a champagne sunset. Well, the resort measures time in sunrises and sunsets, so who are we to argue?

BAROS MALDIVES

MALE, MALDIVES
COORDINATES: (N) 4° 17' 5.3442" (E) 73° 25' 37.6068"

The Maldives is synonymous with honeymoon couples and idyllic tropical islands. Baros Maldives is no exception. Oozing romance and privacy, this small resort is perfect if you want to escape the stresses of everyday life. You can expect total peace and tranquillity. There are no noisy water sports and no children under eight. Now how appealing does that sound?

If that's not enough to tempt you, then the personalised service will win you over. Every aspect of your holiday is focused on making your stay special to you – from a chat with the executive chef over your food preferences, to bespoke dive programmes. Even at the spa, the team will devise a series of treatments, from the plethora of options, especially to suit your needs. It is guaranteed to leave you feeling pampered and relaxed.

The pièce de résistance has to be the house reef that's just a few metres swim from the beach – easily accessible even for timid snorkellers – and bursting with marine life. If you're an experienced diver, there are enough nearby dive sites to explore to keep you happy for at least a week. If you'd prefer not to venture underwater, you won't be missing out, simply pick a spot on your overwater terrace and watch turtles and rays glide past. Or visit the Marine Centre and adopt your own coral and you'll receive an updated picture every six months – a truly unique holiday memory. And we haven't even mentioned the secluded Pool Villas and mouthwatering food – don't leave without enjoying a romantic sandbank dinner.

Above
Crystal-clear waters lap white sandy beaches

Top right
A Baros Premium Pool Villa, shielded by tropical foliage

Bottom right
The Lighthouse Restaurant: cuisine in a unique setting

The wooden veranda of a Beach
Villa leads to a private pool

Above
Well-appointed five-star
luxury is comfortably informal
yet stylishly elegant

Top right
Beach Villas, located along
a meandering coastline, have
spacious interiors

Bottom right
Beach Suites, comprising
a two-bedroom duplex, have
their own rooftop sun deck

80
81
82
83
84
85

MALDIVES

86
87
88
89
90

JUMEIRAH VITTAVELI

SOUTH MALE ATOLL, MALDIVES
COORDINATES: Ⓝ 4° 5′ 59.9994″ Ⓔ 73° 22′ 59.9982″

It's hard to imagine as you arrive at Male International Airport that a 20-minute boat ride is all that lies between you and a haven of utter tranquillity. Nestled on Bolifushi Island in the Maldives is the paradise of Jumeirah Vittaveli.

The first pleasure is settling into your luxurious air-conditioned villa bedecked in pretty, honey-coloured timber. Graced with high ceilings, impeccable decor and state-of-the-art amenities – Apple media centre, flat screen TV and iPod dock – each and every five-star villa feels like home.

The concept embraces an open-space layout, allowing you to take in the stunning sea views and cool breezes wherever you are. Each villa boasts a private pool and personalised wine selection, and the resort enjoys a first-rate spa and three exquisite dining experiences, including Samsara, with its Asian and Maldivian specialities, and Fenesse that sits dreamily overlooking the lagoon waters. Everything is set against pristine white sand beaches and azure Indian Ocean, and is tailor-made to de-stress the weary traveller.

Spend afternoons being massaged at the Talise Spa, learning the virtues of yoga or having fun on the beach with the activities on offer. There's also a fitness centre for the health-conscious and a library to stock up on a few great holiday page-turners to complete the relaxation. A little way along the exclusive resort's beach is the Mu Beach Bar and Grill, a friendly restaurant that dishes up the freshest salads, fish and meat, al fresco under a flawless star-lit sky. A perfect end to another perfect day.

Each beautifully appointed
Beach Revive bedroom
features a deluxe king-size bed

Above
Relax in the shade of a private
veranda with personalised
24-hour butler service

Top right
Mesmerising beauty in a
tranquil setting far from the
pressures of modern life

Bottom right
Beach and Island Revives
have a private pool, garden
and beach

MALDIVES

80
81
82
83
84
85
86
87
88
89
90

JUMEIRAH DHEVANAFUSHI

MERADHOO ISLAND, MALDIVES
COORDINATES: Ⓝ 0° 37' 25.0746" Ⓔ 73° 18' 25.5306"

Jumeirah Dhevanafushi is the ideal place for honeymooners and those seeking a total escape – and it certainly exceeds all its promises.

From the moment you land at Male International Airport, you're pampered by the resort staff and management. The attention to detail is second to none – where else would you be welcomed at the jetty with live music and drinks, topped off with a relaxing foot massage upon arrival at your luxury pad? Set in lush vegetation, there are 13 beachside

Revive villas and eight Island Revives, poised by the azure waters of the Indian Ocean, and a unique Island Sanctuary, nestled amid the flora and scented walkways. The villas are luxuriously spacious and equipped with their own swimming pool and 24-hour butler service. The toughest decision is whether to enjoy the signature spa and bath rituals in the privacy of your own villa or at the extraordinary Talise Spa, suspended over the gently rippling waves.

The food is out of this world with

a wealth of choice from three restaurants – Johara, Mumayaz and Azara – where you may have the rare privilege of seeing your food prepared right in front of you. A memorable experience that's not to be missed is the off-island picnic organised through the resort team. Take a 15-minute speedboat ride to a lovely sand bank and enjoy a picnic lunch with champagne in the middle of the ocean – perfect for contemplating the virtues of getting away from it all.

Below
The sub-tropical resort is located along one of the best beaches in Mauritius

Right
Two-Bedroom Suite Villas offer family accommodation and private pool

MAURITIUS

THE ST. REGIS MAURITIUS

LE MORNE PENINSULA, MAURITIUS
COORDINATES: Ⓢ 20° 27' 21.5208" Ⓔ 57° 18' 42.9834"

Mauritius is as close to paradise on Earth as it gets. The turquoise Indian Ocean is home to extraordinary marine life and the natural landscape benefits from a micro-climate which keeps the weather warm and clement all year round. If you have yet to discover this lush island, 2012 could be your lucky year for, on the UNESCO heritage site of Le Morne, stands the beautiful colonial-style estate that is The St. Regis Mauritius – a bright new arrival.

The St. Regis Mauritius pulls out all the stops for its guests. The properties are synonymous with uncompromising and luxurious refinement, from the flawlessly discreet butler service to the stunningly appointed suites, spa and facilities. In the restaurants, there are collaborations with internationally admired chefs and an award-winning Indian celebrity chef is on site.

The essence of St. Regis hotels across the world is attention to detail. Cherished traditions are alive and well here, like fresh flowers, afternoon tea service, midnight supper, cognac and hand-rolled cigars after dinner or the magnificently theatrical sabering of a champagne bottle by your butler for that special occasion. Staff take great pride in the personal touch the world over – St. Regis has lent its magic to the unique Mauritian blend of a Bloody Mary here.

The surroundings are legendary. The white beaches and the Indian Ocean are overwhelmingly beautiful. You'll simply want to stroll, lounge and daydream along the shore or swim in the cooling depths forever more.

Above
Terrace with a view of the Indian Ocean and beach

Top right
Deluxe bathrooms offer elegance and modern style

Bottom right
Guest rooms are luxurious and look out onto the ocean

Top left
The infinity pool looks out onto palm trees and the Indian Ocean

Bottom left
Presidential Suite Villas are the epitome of discreet refinement

Above
Coast2Coast is an all-day restaurant with a relaxed atmosphere

MARADIVA VILLAS RESORT & SPA

WOLMAR, MAURITIUS
COORDINATES: (S) 20° 17' 44.8794" (E) 57° 21' 53.4666"

If you're searching for the holiday of a lifetime that combines romance, intimacy and authentic character, Maradiva Villas Resort & Spa has it all in spades. A haven of luxury, set in 27 acres of tropical landscape on the west coast of Mauritius, Maradiva prides itself on friendly, discreet service, and a sense of privacy and exclusivity. Each of the 65 guest villas has its own plunge pool and terrace, with adjoining dining and living space, as well as stunning views of the ocean or of the

Food lovers are in for a treat at the Cilantro restaurant which serves a wide selection of Asian specialities, completed by a fabulous Teppanyaki Counter, while the Coast2Coast restaurant offers diverse international cuisine. Both restaurants showcase the freshest and finest produce, sourced directly from the chef's garden. The Breakers Bar is a perfect spot for wiling away the hours in a relaxed environment.
Facilities include water sports, a fitness

in the resort's crown is the Maradiva Spa. Be sure to set a day aside for this award-winning holistic spa that sets new standards in the art of Ayurvedic treatments. The therapists will guide you through these traditional Indian treatments and ancient healing therapies to ensure you come away feeling totally rejuvenated.
We guarantee you'll be planning your next stay here by the time you've checked into your villa on the first day.

MAIA LUXURY RESORT & SPA

ANSE LOUIS MAHE ISLAND, SEYCHELLES
COORDINATES: (S) 4° 42′ 59.7126″ (E) 55°28′ 43.2942″

Privacy and peace is the Maia philosophy and you can really find both in this spectacular resort. A complimentary massage is a great way to begin your stay and ease away stress, followed by free daily yoga and Qi Gong meditation classes. All 30 villas boast dazzling views of the Indian Ocean, which are best enjoyed from the oversized daybeds that grace the spacious accommodation. Spoil the whole family at the blissful open-air Spa, with gorgeous massages for you and fun treatments for the kids – chocolate milk bath anyone? For a thrilling experience why not hire one of the many speedboats available for a tour of the surrounding islands? After an exhausting day of water sports and scuba diving, there's nowhere better to refuel than the Tec-Tec Restaurant, offering the best in Creole and Asian cuisine, with a catch-of-the-day option. For a truly memorable experience why not dine on the beach or under the stars?

Above
The Tec-Tec Restaurant serves gourmet food low in calories

Top right
The Welcome Pavilion is the place to slow down and rest

Bottom right
The Ocean Panoramic Villa sits on the hilltop of the peninsula

Top left
The resort's infinity pool looks out onto the blue waters of the Indian Ocean

Bottom left
The Royal Villa Suite is furnished in contemporary style and features a spacious parlour

Above
Raffles Spa is a perfect haven in which to rejuvinate mind, body and soul

RAFFLES SEYCHELLES

PRASLIN, SEYCHELLES
COORDINATES: Ⓢ 4° 18' 19.3896" Ⓔ 55° 42' 59.3532"

As you arrive at the Raffles Seychelles hotel you're welcomed with open arms by the friendly staff.

It doesn't get better than this – a perfect example of how to blend seamlessly clean, modern architecture into the landscape and exotic vegetation. The beautifully appointed villas look out across staggering views of the ocean from every conceivable angle.

The food is equally spectacular with an excellent choice of fresh fish – don't miss the lobster nights – and fine dishes, all served by attentive staff in beautiful restaurants. And food-allergy sufferers can rest easy here. Diners can alternate between the Losean and the Curieuse restaurants; the Curieuse is great for dining al fresco with its large outdoor space. For breakfast, the chef will rustle up off-the-menu treats and, for late refreshments, don't miss out on the Praslin Sling or Passion Fruit Mojito, both delicious signature cocktails.

The spa area and gym are located on a lovely walkway, and offer luxurious pampering treatments.

If the Seychelles are on your wish list, then you really must consider this extraordinary new Raffles hotel.

NORTH ISLAND

NORTH ISLAND, SEYCHELLES
COORDINATES: Ⓢ 4° 23'40.54" Ⓔ 55° 15'0.97"

When you dream of a tropical paradise what images spring to mind? An island covered in palm trees and exotic foliage, surrounded by white sandy beaches and crystal-clear waters teeming with marine life. A Noah's Ark where endangered endemic animals are given a refuge for regeneration. Individual thatched-roof lodges hidden among the greenery where you can play at being Robinson Crusoe. Well, this is North Island. It may sound cliched and it's an exhausted phrase, but "barefoot luxury" perfectly sums up this heavenly escape – at one with nature, yet unashamedly aimed at providing the very best in location and privacy, accommodation and facilities. Aside from the sheer physical beauty, there is so much on North Island to fall in love with – the space and privacy of the villas, each designed to blend in with the natural surroundings, the freedom to walk barefoot or jump on a bicycle and picnic on a deserted beach, the "any menu, any venue, anytime" philosophy giving you the ability to choose your own menu and decide when and where to eat it, and of course the island's resident, and individually named, giant tortoises. And we haven't even touched on the impeccable service, unbeatable diving and magical spa.

So throw caution to the wind and experience life as Robinson Crusoe, stranded on a tropical island, albeit in a luxurious and ultra comfortable way.

Above
Guests feel extra-special staying in the Presidential Villa

Top right
North Island Villas where guests can commune with nature

Bottom right
Villas are a space to free the mind and refresh the soul

KASBAH DU TOUBKAL

IMLIL, MOROCCO
COORDINATES: Ⓝ 31° 7' 56.3196" Ⓦ 7° 55' 9.0438"

Getting away from it all can sometimes mean a long and dusty journey. But, as Polly Crossman discovered, a trip to a distant Kasbah can be well worth the effort

Top
Garden House Suites look out onto the peak of Jbel Toubkal

Bottom
Suite bedrooms offer North African style and restful comfort

Right
Kasbah du Toubkal is situated at the foot of North Africa's highest peak

I had to come a long way into the Atlas Mountains to finally find the moment, after many years, when I honestly enjoyed a cup of tea.

The 1997 Peugeot had groaned to a halt, crunching over a gravelly surface. "Appens all ze time," mumbled the driver in a thick French accent, stepping out from behind the wheel, a half-lit cigarette hanging from the corner of his mouth. "We wait." We've not broken down but a road block is in our path – the makeshift kind, with ticker tape strung between dusty old plastic chairs and guarded by a small moustachioed man with slicked hair and a khaki suit. Such is the madness of Morocco.

Sinking into my seat, I enjoy being still for a minute. After the weaving between lorries and mopeds and motorbikes, heavy with pens of chickens and families of four clinging on as we'd zoomed out of Marrakech, heading due south for the High Atlas, my tummy is tender.

Following the driver out onto the edge of the road, the air is refreshing and clear, the kind you'll have missed in the city. We've swapped city for desert, jam-packed streets for open landscapes. The weather is big. There's a hint of moisture about, repelling the dustiness through which we've come, but also warning of a microclimate that could change dramatically in just five minutes or so. The feeling grows with altitude, with the kind of brooding that could turn an afternoon of rhapsody lounging on the roof terrace at the

Kasbah, into a torrent of expletives as the clouds break and roll.

The queue of traffic lengthens behind. For a while, the mountain air has calmed the chaos, negating the shouting and blaring of city traffic. But then the train of patience wears thin, the horns fall into their usual orchestra and the khaki-clad guy gives in, waving us past the perforated pipe that's kept the crowd at bay.

The car carries forward on tenterhooks, clutching at balance on its axel and swinging through bends at an alarming rate. We turn left in the village of Asni – near enough the sole direction required from Marrakech, a mere 40km away – into the last 17km of the journey and driving until the road runs out.

We roll into Imlil, where a melee of locals hanging out on plastic chairs greets us with welcoming eyes and toothy grins. The mules are waiting too and I wince in tandem with the beast lumped with my suitcase. There can't be many places where the reception is a ten- minute mule ride from your room, but the trip completes the transition from civilisation to the middle of nowhere.

Inside the heavy wooden door and yellowy walls, harmony rules. Crocuses and irises are creeping into bloom amid terracotta pots and an abundance of greenery, hinting at the carpet of spring flowers that will transform the surrounding slopes within weeks. We're met by the charming Hajj Maurice and his wife

Hammam: a traditional
bathing retreat to rejuvenate
tired limbs after a long trek
in the mountains

Hajja Arkia, managers of the Kasbah and immensely proud of their patch. Around them, other staff babble in Berber, in perfect pitch with the bubble of the river.

Inside there are teetering piles of oranges ripe for juicing, bowls of fresh walnuts and a gigantic wood-burning stove, stoked high and throwing out heat. The sun has dipped behind the mountains and the clouds have followed us in, obscuring snowy peaks and quickly dropping the temperature. Combined with under-floor heating taking the edge off the tiles, the roaring fire hints at the authentic luxury that characterises the whole place.

The beds are low and soft, and loaded with blankets, the bathtub deep and long, and there are well-worn pairs of leather slippers to slope around in – great for recovering from long days of trekking. A balcony that runs the length of our Garden House, with carefully positioned deckchairs, hints at the views that will greet us by day, as well as some spectacular stargazing. The dusky light doesn't last long and soon the cherry-blossomed valley is flooded with black, leaving strings of lanterns to light rickety pathways. Scooping the bottle of red that's been warming by the fire – the Kasbah has no licence, but guests are encouraged to bring their own drink with them – we nip up to the restaurant with woolly jumpers to block out the chill.

Made cosy by curios and candlelight, and with low-slung tables and Moroccan couches, the restaurant lends itself to satisfying mountain appetites over long, shared suppers. We're welcomed with a traditional rose water hand wash, before tearing still-warm loaves of bread and demolishing bowls of thick vegetable soup and a huge lamb tagine, all made with local produce and the day's forage from the Kasbah garden. There's no menu as such, just three courses of proper homemade fare that warms you through to your toes.

Over dinner, Mike McHugo tells us how it took more than five years for him and his brother Chris to secure permission to restore the crumbling Kasbah, yet alone build his vision of a mountain retreat. Since 1994, buildings have been reworked and added, fostering a feel that it's stood firm for centuries through local craftsmanship and meticulous attention to detail.

The Kasbah is run through a unique partnership with the surrounding community, whereby a 5 per cent levy on room bills is channelled back into the village – a mark of the Kasbah's commitment to its people and an indication of just how down to earth the place is, even 1,800 metres up in the clouds. The McHugo's filial passion for this part of North Africa oozes from every inch of every wall.

By the time I roll to bed, satiated and sleepy, a hot water bottle has stolen between my sheets.

Rising with the birdsong and rushing water, I'm as eager as a child on Christmas morning to peer out of the window. I'm not disappointed. There, in all of her 4,167-metre glory, is Jbel Toubkal, standing tall and proud bang in the middle of the valley.

After my breakfast of pancakes, fresh honey and fig jam, I was being measured for a walking pole – begrudgingly, you know, in the same way that I thought I could also power through without a handmade straw hat. But four hours later when my legs have taken a hammering and the sun has singed the end of my nose, I had to hand it to our guide Omar, patient and reserved, that he had known what he was talking about. He seemed to know the mountain like the back of his hand, picking paths out of nowhere and cutting back between goat herders. I should have known that his weather-worn features were a sign of years of walking and calves of steel. He told tales of walking these trails since he could remember and walking two hours to a grassy plateau that we pass for inter-village football tournaments. Bringing up the rear a mule follows quietly, treading his own path and never straying far, carrying water and a supply of apples and dates that save the day when we risk tiring. The walking is challenging, but not overly difficult – the perfect balance of puff and big views, with plenty of time to drink the whole thing in.

We eventually reach the Azzaden Trekking Lodge, the Kasbah's second outpost. There are rooms here that are basic yet cosy, designed for trekkers staying out in the mountains. Maurice tailors treks according to the strengths and ambitions of his walkers, stretching to more than five days in the High Atlas, with stops at the lodge and camp sites – the ascent of Toubkal is feasible in two days for anyone with a decent level of fitness.

Dining Room: a Moroccan menu, featuring fresh local produce, is served in atmospheric surroundings

Further rounds of home-cooked fare await us and a balcony drenched in sunshine made for these kinds of lunches. The lodge seems to cling to the hillside, along with the neighbouring buildings, all perched on precipices amid cows and crops growing on terraces, but perfectly positioned for the panoramas.

A rocky – to say the least – jeep ride on dirt tracks carved into mountainsides eventually delivered us back to the Kasbah, saved from being utterly terrifying by the grace of views stretching for miles through valleys and villages.

The Kasbah is more of a haven than ever on our return and the bath works its magic, soothing sore knees. Cursing the sunburn that had appeared on the backs of my hands, I was dehydrated. And that's when the tea arrived – not just any old tea, but proper, loose leaf peppermint tea poured from a height out of a silver pot into a delicate glass in the sunshine on the roof of the Kasbah du Toubkal.

I settled into my deckchair and ordered another pot.

MOROCCO

UGANDA

Top left
Safari eco-lodges respect the African environment

Bottom left
Western comfort is balanced by local needs

Above
Accommodation is eco-friendly and intimate

VOLCANOES KYAMBURA GORGE LODGE

KYAMBURA GORGE, UGANDA
COORDINATES: Ⓢ 0° 12' 28.9002" Ⓔ 30° 6' 2.2644"

If you long to see majestic lions loping across the savannah, crafty crocodiles basking in muddy waters and chimpanzees swooping through the canopy, be sure to make Kyambura Gorge Lodge your chosen safari stop. The Lodge stands on the edge of the Kyambura Gorge and Queen Elizabeth National Park, the misty peaks of the Rwenzori Mountains just visible in the distance. Rich with wildlife, the park boasts big cats, elephants, hippos and nine types of monkey, not to mention 600 species of birds.

The dramatic Kyambura Gorge, at the edge of the park, is home to a threatened community of chimpanzees. Follow the knowledgeable guides through the forest to observe these fascinating animals.

Staying in one of the uniquely furnished bandas, fashioned into the hillside and complete with luxurious bathrooms, is definitely the best way to enjoy the astonishing views from this Lodge. In the evenings, the Omumashaka Drama Group bring Uganda's colourful culture to life. But watching the chimps and big game in this untouched habitat is a memory you'll cherish long after you've left Kyambura.

ABU CAMP

OKAVANGO DELTA, BOTSWANA
COORDINATES: Ⓢ 19° 59' 39.0078" Ⓔ 23° 25' 6.2394"

Abu Camp simply has to be on your list of places to visit if you're a fan of elephants. Where else can you actually become part of an African elephant herd and get a glimpse of their world? As you walk with and ride the elephants, you'll get to know the personalities of each family member. The playful baby elephants are adorable. You can even sleep among them, under the stars, overlooking the elephant boma. How amazing to drift off to sleep listening to the low snores and contented rumblings of the elephants below.

Abu provides the very best in privacy, location, accommodation and service, while respecting the environment. As all visitors are able to be absorbed into a whole new world, the camp works as a haven of peace and tranquillity, immersed within the natural rhythms of the bush. The camp is considered to be beyond five-star rating, with each unit's stylish furnishings and fittings individually chosen for every room. The dining experience is of the highest standard with internationally trained chefs, who provide creative cuisine, served alfresco on the

deck, along with an extensive wine selection and a nightcap at the end of the day round the campfire. The combination of a unique safari and the breathtaking wilderness area of the Okavango Delta, the imaginative yet luxurious tented accommodation, complete with copper bathtubs, the mouthwatering cuisine – bush picnics are a highlight – and, of course, the elephants themselves, make for a humbling and rewarding, once-in-a-lifetime experience.

Above
Tented rooms blend in seamlessly with the natural surroundings

Top right
A lounge area for reflection and relaxation amid the African bush

Bottom right
Bedrooms are light and airy with stylish furnishings and fittings

Top left
Big cats in the Mara are a wonderful sight on the rugged plains of Africa

Bottom left
A luxurious tented suite, including bathroom, is real comfort on safari

Above
Best game viewing in the Masai Mara, right on the banks of the Mara River

GOVERNORS' IL MORAN CAMP

MASAI MARA GAME RESERVE, KENYA
COORDINATES: (S) 1° 16′ 56.8632″ (E) 35° 2′ 11.148″

Governors' Il Moran Camp lies in a corner of the Masai Mara known as the best wildlife real estate in the world and which is famous for its abundance of wildlife all year round. This extraordinary, luxury tented camp is shaded by a forest on the banks of the Mara River where herds of game and families of elephants roam majestically by to drink from the river. Rather endearingly, it's also not uncommon to fall asleep to the sounds of a chomping hippo feeding on the grass by your tent. It's safe to say that Il Moran Camp has maintained the atmosphere of the original hunting camp, but with the bonus of luxury and comfort thrown in for very good measure. The guides are the best there is and, whether you choose to explore from the comfort of a custom-built safari vehicle, on foot or from the heights of a hot-air balloon, they'll ensure you have the fullest and most sumptuous experience. Nothing conquers hearts like the thrill of a hot-air balloon safari as the sun begins to rise. Floating silently over the Mara River, the forest and the plains is a breathtaking feeling, topped off with a champagne breakfast on landing. With 40 years' experience, the Il Moran Camp safari is second to none. Where else can you relax in an en-suite bathroom, sink into your olive-wood knotted bed after a day in the bush and dream of Africa?

LOISABA WILDERNESS

LAIKIPIA, KENYA
COORDINATES: Ⓝ 0° 1' 0.0012" Ⓔ 37° 4' 0.0012"

Loisaba is a 61,000-acre private conservation area that makes for a very different safari adventure. It lies on the edge of a sheer escarpment, looking out across the Laikipia plateau and surrounding landscapes towards Mount Kenya. The tapestry of forest, canyon and plain offer a haven for the extraordinary wildlife – ideal for guests hoping to observe wild animals in their natural habitat. Guests can enjoy game viewing in total safety as all accommodation opens out onto private verandahs, which overlook a nearby waterhole.

There is a variety of luxury lodgings, namely Loisaba House, Loisaba Cottage, Loisaba Lodge and Star Beds, all packed with a "wow" factor. Loisaba House and Cottage take the safari experience to new heights – self-contained and opulent in style, with their own swimming pool, staff, vehicle(s) and guide(s). Star Beds offer a chance to be hosted by the Laikipiak Maasai and experience a unique form of star-gazing. You spend a night out under the stars, listening to the sounds of the African night and get to watch the sunrise from the comfort of a cosy double bed – a remarkable experience. We recommend combining a few nights in both types of accommodation to get a full sense of being on safari. What better way to get from your house to your Star Bed than by being whisked away on horseback or by Land Rover? It's worth noting that by staying at Loisaba, guests contribute to its conservation, as well as to the long-term future of the people living in the area.

KENYA

Above
An African-style bedroom at the House, a self-contained private residence

Top right
The House has an infinity pool perched on the edge of an escarpment

Bottom right
Star Beds offer an unforgettable night under the African stars

Pezula Resort Hotel & Spa,
Private Estate, Noetzie Beach

Above
The Castle has direct access to one of South Africa's top-three beaches

Top right
Peaceful bedrooms have private terraces with views of the Indian Ocean

Bottom right
Sumptuous bathrooms pamper guests in comfort and five-star style

SOUTH AFRICA

102
103
104
105
106
107
108
109

PEZULA PRIVATE CASTLE

KNYSNA, SOUTH AFRICA
COORDINATES: (S) 34° 4' 12.2442" (E) 23° 5' 21.7788"

Ever wondered what it would be like to stay in a fairy-tale castle? Well Pezula Private Castle holds the answer. Sitting on the eastern head of Knysna on South Africa's Garden Route Coast and surrounded by rugged cliffs, ancient forests and sheltered beaches, the setting is indeed the stuff of fairy tales. The views over Pezula Championship Golf Course, the Indian Ocean and the Knysna Lagoon are magical, and set the tone for a remarkable stay.
The 78 stylish suites are housed in detached villas, and feature many home comforts, like a fireplace, lovely for a cosy nightcap, a private balcony and spacious bathroom fit for a king.
The main building is a great place to relax or mix with other guests, with plenty of places to explore, like the sumptuous cigar lounge, champagne and whisky bar, library, wine cellar and two gourmet restaurants. On Friday and Saturday evenings, the region's finest produce is served at Zachary's restaurant, while Pezula's latest dining venue, Café Z, is open seven days a week. Café Z is more informal and relaxed, but equally refined. Romantic highlights are the boma dinners in a rustic, thatched summer house where guests can dine, under the African sky, on gourmet picnic hampers supplied by Café Z – also perfect for day trips out.
For extra indulgence, visit the spa after a day of canoeing, hiking or golf. Or treat yourself to a stay in ultra-luxurious accommodation on Noetzie Beach, complete with dedicated butler and chef.

SOUTH AFRICA

102
103
104
105
106
107
108
109

Top left
Guest suites offer luxurious refinement and the opulence of a bygone age

Bottom left
The Royal Suite deck looks out onto a private game reserve in Africa's Bushveld

Above
Royal Malewane is situated close to South Africa's Kruger National Park

ROYAL MALEWANE

THE GREATER KRUGER AREA, SOUTH AFRICA
COORDINATES: Ⓢ 24° 31'08.00" Ⓔ 31° 09'43.00"

Royal Malewane is one of Africa's most luxurious wildlife lodges, renowned for providing the pinnacle of luxury "Big-Five" game viewing. Set in a canopy of indigenous acacia and lantern bush trees, the six luxury suites, each with its own rich wooden deck, rim-flow pool and thatched gazebo, are linked by walkways that thread to the main lodge. The Royal and Malewane Suites comfortably accommodate four guests each, with the complimentary services of a butler and private chef, plus up to four complimentary massages per

Surrounded by the untamed African bush, the Waters of Royal Malewane Bush Spa is perfect for guests seeking relaxation or rejuvenation. This sanctuary for the senses comprises an indoor and outdoor treatment area, gym, double treatment rooms with spa baths and a Vichy shower, four casitas for post-treatment relaxation, and a 25-metre heated lap pool. Treatments are inspired by African rituals, using indigenous oils and traditional ingredients.

ELLERMAN HOUSE

CAPE TOWN, SOUTH AFRICA
COORDINATES: Ⓢ 33° 55' 44.79" Ⓔ 18° 22' 40.46"

It must be said that Ellerman House is the most breathtaking location in Cape Town. Resting on the slopes of Bantry Bay, this gorgeous property enjoys sweeping views of the shimmering Atlantic Ocean and the V&A Waterfront, which are only ten minutes' drive away.

Greeted by the warm and hospitable staff, guests surrender every care to the concierge team who make your stay unforgettable with tailor-made discovery packages of the city, region and the rich local culture. With just nine bedrooms and two suites, there's a wonderful feeling of intimacy at

Ellerman House that makes it extra special. There's also the spectacular Ellerman Villa for those seeking utter seclusion in a two-storey private haven complete with butler service.

No detail is too small. Breakfast includes home-baked breads, pastries and freshly pressed juices, meals on the extraordinary terrace provide the perfect blend of romance and fine cuisine, laundry is elegantly hand-wrapped in tissue paper, and the Ellerman Spa has three treatment rooms and state-of-the art facilities. In true Relais & Châteaux style, magical touches include a dazzling 7,500-strong

wine selection available with dinner at the residence – any wine lover's dream. As if this wasn't incredible enough, the property is home to a comprehensive collection of 20th-century South African art throughout, while the private Ellerman Contemporary gallery showcases the best of South African modern art.

But it's the genuine attention from staff here that remains with you. Their pride in this extraordinary location is palpable and contagious. Memories of your stay will have you counting down the days until you return to Ellerman House.

Above
The Spa offers a wide range of relaxing and beautifying treatments

Top right
The Ellerman Villa Lilac Room opens onto a balcony with ocean views

Bottom right
The Sea View Room is peaceful, luxurious and well-equipped

Indulge in late-night lounging
at Kensington Place

Above
Pool patio: indoor and outdoor
living blends effortlessly

Top right
Lounge patio: modern comfort
defined by attention to detail

Bottom right
Bedroom: king-size, restful,
well-appointed luxury

102
103
104
105
106
107

SOUTH AFRICA

108
109

KENSINGTON
PLACE

CAPE TOWN, SOUTH AFRICA
COORDINATES: **S** 33° 56' 22.0518" **E** 18° 24' 18.396"

One of Cape Town's pioneering small boutique hotels, Kensington Place prefers to be known as a private hotel. It has a designer's eye and elegant urban escapism stamped all over it. It offers the right environment for a flawless experience of Cape Town and all this beautiful city has to offer. Situated on the slopes of Table Mountain, in the leafy suburb of Higgovale, the hotel is peaceful yet only a stone's throw from the city centre and its hotspots. The design and ambience marry plush textures and contemporary detail with chic intimacy – there are just eight rooms. The staff are obliging and helpful. They recommend the best places to eat or day trips and take time to make you feel special.

The bar is open all hours and food is served practically all day – excellent for a late-night snack. You can relax by the pool, treat yourself with the wonderful toiletry products in your bathroom, or arrange for a massage or a sports session (there's a complimentary membership at a nearby gym). The lounge area has a cosy fireplace for after-dinner relaxation and, should you need to stay connected, there's free wi-fi and an in-room laptop at your disposal, as well as a library of films and music to enjoy. You'll sleep like a baby in your Egyptian cotton sheets ready for the next day and that sun-kissed balcony breakfast. Kensington Place is lauded by global travel experts, but don't take our word for it – try it for yourself.

Private Granite Suite: an
outside riverview bath for an
authentic African experience

102
103
104
105
106
107
108
109

SOUTH AFRICA

Above
Londolozi game drives:
true wildlife safaris for
discerning guests

Top right
Pioneer Camp candlelit
dinner by the pool: fine cuisine
and exceptional service

Bottom right
Pioneer Suite: family
accommodation or
a romantic getaway

LONDOLOZI GAME RESERVE

MPUMALANGA, SOUTH AFRICA
COORDINATES: Ⓢ 24° 48' 40.9968" Ⓔ 31° 30' 16.6032"

One of the oldest family-run, stand-alone operations, Londolozi Game Reserve is the best-known of the Kruger private reserves and home to one of the most epic safaris in the world. Extending over 17,000 hectares, this prime game reserve is renowned for its exceptional leopard viewing, vast open spaces and encounters with the big five of the African bush. You'll meet people who live together in a utopia of gentle smiles and life-affirming handshakes.

Situated on the Sand River in the very heart of the Sabi Sands Game Reserve, Londolozi knows how to juxtapose the big outdoors with some of the most exhilarating private spaces on the continent. Located just metres from the action, Pioneer Camp and Tree Camp are part of the world-famous Relais & Chateaux hotel group, while Varty Camp and Founders Camp are perfect for a family safari. But all lodges have spectacular views and modish interiors, and offer effortless service and the very best in African living.

For the ultimate stay, choose one of the Granite Suites, featuring outdoor river-view baths that achieve a seamless integration with nature through large doors and windows which open directly onto the river. Your experience will be discreet and playful, infused with all the romanticism of a Hemingway adventure, screened by the beautiful Riverine Forest. Come here for the adrenaline of a hot day in the bush, sporadic laughter in the plunge pools at twilight and, perhaps, for a candlelit feast under the African stars.

MIDDLE EAST, ASIA & PACIFIC

Bab Al Yam poolside café restaurant provides informal and alfresco dining

UNITED ARAB EMIRATES

112
113

114
115
116
117

Above
The iconic hotel, designed like a billowing sail, dominates Dubai architecture

Top right
Al Mahara restaurant serves the finest seafood and features an exotic aquarium

Bottom right
The Royal Suite is stately and opulent with lavish interiors – the last word in luxury

BURJ AL ARAB

DUBAI, UNITED ARAB EMIRATES
COORDINATES: Ⓝ 25° 8' 27.1422" Ⓔ 55° 11' 9.4452"

Burj Al Arab is the jewel in the crown of Dubai's luxurious and fashionable landmarks. Its striking exterior resembles the billowing sail of an Arabian dhow soaring high above a man-made island just off Jumeirah Beach.

The accommodation is quite spectacular and spacious with lounges and dining areas, kitchens and offices. All are duplex suites with floor-to-ceiling windows looking out onto the glittering Gulf waters. As expected many of the suites are dazzling in their display of gold finishing – for a regal experience the Royal Suite is richly decked in glorious colour with four-poster bed.

There are lovely touches like complimentary beach bag and sandals in the rooms but, for the pièce de résistance, turn-down is a real treat with little gifts left on the pillow, like a purse-sized Hermes perfume. Staff tend to your every need and pride themselves on their friendly and professional discretion, be it around the pool or in your room, bringing you drinks and refreshments or handling your random personal requests in true butler fashion.

There's an aquarium-style Al Mahara restaurant that matches the standard set by its unique style with perfect seafood. The choice is large though with six other dining options, as well as the SkyView Bar for a super nightcap. Your stay won't be complete without an indulgent moment at the spa, so be sure to book into the Assawan Spa & Health Club that offers an Around-the-World massage that includes shiatsu, and Balinese, Swedish and Thai techniques.

Top left
Armani Fountain Suites
have stunning views
of The Dubai Fountain

Bottom left
Living room of an expansive
Armani Ambassador Suite

Above
The Lobby is a smart
café serving traditional
and creative coffees

ARMANI HOTEL DUBAI

DUBAI, UNITED ARAB EMIRATES
COORDINATES: Ⓝ 25° 11' 49.6998" Ⓔ 55° 16' 26.799"

Armani Hotel Dubai is the first hotel designed by Giorgio Armani, and is the epitome of style and taste. The fashion designer has brought the essence of Italian chic to this hotel, housed in the world's tallest building, Burj Khalifa, soaring above downtown Dubai with commanding views of the city and its glittering skyline.

Guests are treated to a veritable lifestyle experience with aesthetically stunning signature suites and rooms, an excellent choice of seven innovative restaurants, exclusive boutiques, the first in-hotel Armani/SPA and,

crucially, a team of round-the-clock Lifestyle Managers, part of the "Stay with Armani" philosophy that ensures a home-away-from-home experience. Armani Hotels & Resorts strongly believe that travel is as much an emotional journey as a physical one and, as a result, each hotel guest is assigned a personal Lifestyle Manager. Think of this as a personal contact and host, from the moment you book your room to check-out and beyond. Nothing is too much trouble. You need someone to give you the best addresses in Dubai, fix you a meal in the middle of the night or take care of your laundry – no worries, it's all arranged in the blink of an eye.

This hotel is so much more than a luxurious, stylish and elegant holiday and business destination. It has been meticulously designed and laid out by Giorgio Armani himself, with guests' comfort in mind at all times. This means that every detail, from the bespoke furnishings to restaurant menus and in-room amenities, are the fruit of painstaking planning and an appreciation of guests' emotional reactions. The plan has been plainly successful, as you will agree reclining on your king-size bed and looking out at the uninterrupted view of the landmark Dubai Fountain, outside your window. The seven hotel restaurants cater for all tastes and include a selection of world cuisines, ranging from Japanese and Indian to Mediterranean and authentic Italian fine dining. Also popular among guests are the three exclusive retail outlets: Armani/Galleria, the first and only place in Dubai where the Giorgio Armani/Privé Collection is showcased; Armani/Dolci, a luxurious confectionary store offering a selection of chocolates and more; and Armani/Fiori, a floral boutique with exquisite fresh flower arrangements and vases exclusively designed by Giorgio Armani.

Relaxation and pampering the senses are taken very seriously here too and, as a result, the hotel has introduced the Armani/SPA that offers fully tailored sensory experiences which suit individual needs. Each unique space in the Armani/SPA provides a context for personalised treatments, personal fitness and sequential thermal bathing, as well as for private and social relaxation.

Downtown Dubai, described as "The Centre of Now", is the place to be, with the hotel just walking distance from The Dubai Mall, the world's largest shopping and entertainment destination. But the chances are you won't stray too far from the serenity of the Armani Hotel Dubai.

112
113
114
115

UNITED ARAB EMIRATES

116
117

Left
Savour the best of regional Italian cuisine, served with Armani style

Above
The exclusive Armani/Privé lounge hosts exciting nights in Dubai

112
113
114
115
116
117

UNITED ARAB EMIRATES

Top left
The pool at dusk is a
haven of tranquillity
against Dubai's skyline

Bottom left
The hotel and grounds
are a statement of
luxury and splendour

Above
The Palace Collection
offers comfort and a
warm welcome

KEMPINSKI HOTEL & RESIDENCES PALM JUMEIRAH

DUBAI, UNITED ARAB EMIRATES
COORDINATES: Ⓝ 25° 6' 43.6428" Ⓔ 55° 6' 33.3612"

Kempinski Hotel and Residences Palm Jumeirah is as extravagant in design as in its address, enjoying the ultimate in exclusive locations – a genuine island getaway at Palm Jumeirah.

Views of the Arabian Sea and Palm Jumeirah lagoon, plus Dubai's glittering skyline, are breathtaking, In fact, this destination is unique to the region and possesses a truly European boutique feel in its architecture and ambience. Suites, penthouses and villas, courtesy

yet plush. While the restaurants and bars resemble European palaces and seaside retreats with verdant gardens. Good news for purists who appreciate old-world etiquette is that service and food also reflect a well-observed love of tradition and variety.

Luxury abounds throughout. All accommodation has a terrace and many of the suites, penthouses and villas boast a private pool or outdoor Jacuzzi, which makes watching the sun

It's safe to say that nothing is lacking here, least of all glamour. Living spaces are a home-away-from-home, and are thoughtfully equipped with the latest technology for wizard-like access to the internet, films and music. And there's in-room dining with the 24-hour Palace Ceremony service. Whether you're a gourmet food lover, a water sports fan, in need of spa relief or looking to relax in style with your family, everything is done with

THE ST. REGIS SAADIYAT

ABU DHABI, UNITED ARAB EMIRATES
COORDINATES: Ⓝ 24° 32' 28.0278" Ⓔ 54° 25' 31.0548"

Saadiyat Island is a place of staggering natural beauty. It's no surprise that hawksbill turtles find refuge in its pristine white sands or that bottlenose dolphins play in the surf along its shoreline. What's more, its location is ideal for guests in search of peace, just 20 minutes from Abu Dhabi International Airport and minutes from downtown Abu Dhabi.

Now there's a new jewel sparkling on the island's horizon and it's The St. Regis Saadiyat Island Resort, Abu Dhabi. Eagerly anticipated for the legendary St. Regis signature of American ingenuity and European hospitality, this luxury resort brings its own touch of Mediterranean and Middle-Eastern colour to the experience. The St. Regis tradition of intuitive butler service is all-pervasive with attentive staff who cater for your every need, from complimentary in-room drinks to packing your suitcase for your journey home.

The hotel's natural environment breathes warmth into the decor throughout the resort's living spaces that range from the intimate Superior Rooms and Suites to the majestic Royal Suite, each with its own private balcony. Unique to this location are the stunning Iridium Spa, The St. Regis Athletic Club – a state-of-the-art gym – the Regal Ballroom for private events, and the exclusive Sandcastle Club where one to 12 year olds are entertained with indoor and outdoor activities.

The dazzling choice of restaurants and lounge areas, many with perfect views, reflect the welcoming and refined atmosphere of this stunning venue. It has to be seen to be believed.

Above
The Resort is framed by an 18-hole golf course designed by Gary Player

Top right
Mediterranean architecture is enhanced with the use of natural materials

Bottom right
Mediterranean style is continued with warm and welcoming interiors throughout

Below
The Lobby's dazzlingly vivid modern interior extends a warm welcome

Right
The Extreme WOW Suite has a style of its own, in a league of its own

W DOHA HOTEL & RESIDENCES

DOHA, QATAR
COORDINATES: Ⓝ 25° 19' 43.2444" Ⓔ 51° 31' 49.0008"

If you have ever stayed in a W hotel you'll know that there are a multitude of positive expressions used to describe them. The philosophy and superior quality of service and style come before the hotel brand name, not the other way round. Let's start with design – a crucial part of a guest's first impressions. The W Doha Hotel & Residences is the city's first lifestyle-design hotel that won't disappoint even the most seasoned business traveller. With a striking exterior of shining surfaces and gleaming glass, it's a cutting-edge blend of lights, colours and indigenous materials. You enter a world where luxury and slick service are delivered with a smile which sets the scene for your entire stay. You'll receive a complimentary drink at check-in, while your bags are taken to your room. Staff take every opportunity to make you

the 24-hour signature Whatever/Whenever® concierge service. The accommodation is sophisticated with 441 guest rooms, suites and residences of varying size and configuration, including rooms specifically adapted for reduced-mobility guests. The interior is characteristically innovative with some incredible technological features, from LCD TVs to iPod cradles, and quirky details like a fully stocked munchies box with delicious goodies to enjoy. Three stylish lounges include the signature W Living Room experience, Wahm modern poolside lounge, and the ultra-fashionable Crystal which serves cocktails while international DJs play the latest sounds.
There's an embarrassment of riches when it comes to food. The three-star Michelin chef Jean-Georges Vongerichten works his magic in two of W Doha's restaurants. First,

Market, dotted with clusters of custom lanterns to add to the exotic ambience and where the menu is inspired by the street food found in South-East Asia. And then there's Market by Jean-Georges which blends international cuisine with local Arabian flavours. Elsewhere, the prestigious La Maison du Caviar serves the world's most exquisite caviars and the best of French bistro cuisine. For after-dinner coffee, the chic W Café is a lovely spot – also good for business or to just get away from it all.
Exclusive features to add to W Doha's attraction are the region's only Bliss Spa, SWEAT® which is a state-of-the-art fitness facility, and WET®, a glamorous temperature-controlled pool. From now on, when in Qatar, W Doha Hotel & Residences is the only place to stay.

THE ST. REGIS DOHA

DOHA, QATAR
COORDINATES: Ⓝ 25° 21' 1.0908" Ⓔ 51° 31' 41.5056"

Doha, the capital city of Qatar, is a vital centre for so many industries and is home to some of the region's most dynamic businesses. It will also be welcoming thousands of new residents of The Pearl and Lusail City. And at the heart of this energetic city is the luxurious haven of The St. Regis Doha hotel.

This globally recognised hotel brand is respected for its tradition of impeccable round-the-clock butler service. Guests are treated like royalty while little details, like fresh flowers in rooms, are part and parcel of the overall approach.

There's a fabulous treat in store for everyone who stays at the hotel – all guests get a private butler for the duration of their stay. Any request you may have, from your suit being pressed to a last-minute gift for a loved one, will be tailored to match your specific requirements and tastes. It makes for a memorable experience.

Then again there are so many unforgettable moments – delicious menus from all over the world and a dazzling choice of restaurants, courtesy of more than 100 culinary staff. Guest rooms and suites feature elegant custom-made furnishings, with silk wall coverings and antiques that create a luxury home-from-home feeling. All this is topped off with sparkling views of the tranquil Arabian Gulf and a private beach to watch the sunset on yet another perfect day.

Above
Interiors feature contemporary design and modern styling

Top right
All 336 guest rooms and suites offer comfort and convenience

Bottom right
The hotel is located on the beachfront of the Arabian Gulf

Top left
The exclusive facilities of Al Husn (The Castle) include an infinity pool and private beach

Bottom left
CHI, The Spa is the largest and most luxurious of its kind in the Sultanate of Oman

Above
Al Bandar Hotel Piano Lounge is perfect for an aperitif, late-night cocktail or cognac

SHANGRI-LA'S BARR AL JISSAH RESORT & SPA

MUSCAT, OMAN
COORDINATES: N 23° 33' 9.6156" E 58° 39' 37.3608"

Where else can you request the resort's dedicated Turtle Ranger to alert you when there's action from the resident nesting turtles, giving you time to head to the beach with your family to watch? This is just one of the family-friendly activities you can experience at Shangri-La's Barr Al Jissah Resort & Spa. Kids will

But it's not simply a resort for families. CHI, The Spa is an adults-only haven of peace, and the Al Husn area of the resort is exclusively for adults, with its own private – and peaceful – infinity pool and beach.

It may sound cliched, but this resort really does offer something for everyone. With its extensive facilities

OMAN

Top left
The Watergarden Courtyard features traditional Omani architecture

Bottom left
The exclusive Long Pool is simply world-class

Above
Handsomely appointed Deluxe Rooms offer style and relaxation

THE CHEDI MUSCAT

MUSCAT, OMAN
COORDINATES: Ⓝ 23° 36' 7.1562" Ⓔ 58° 23' 55.017"

Surrounded by the majestic Hajar Mountains and the crystal waters of the Gulf of Oman, The Chedi Muscat glimmers like a pearl on a private beach. Twenty one acres of manicured gardens, with charming ponds and water features, complement the perfect mix of Omani architecture and a profound Asian Zen style, creating an incredibly relaxing ambience in elegantly understated surroundings. The Chedi Muscat is famous for its blissful spa, the largest in Muscat. Try the two-handed Jade massage to relieve your stresses and strains.

With six amazing restaurants, the biggest dilemma is which one to choose. You're spoilt for choice, with traditional Arabic flavours to spicy Indian curries, impossibly fresh seafood and fragrant Asian dishes. Naturally, The Chedi's opulence extends poolside. Savour a glass of iced mint and lemon water as you lounge by one of the three glorious infinity pools. The remarkable Long Pool completely lives up to its name and the Serai Pool welcomes families with children.

TAJ FALAKNUMA PALACE

HYDERABAD, INDIA
COORDINATES: Ⓝ 17° 19' 51.528" Ⓔ 78° 28' 1.5846"

If you feel like retracing the steps of native Nizam rulers in majestic style, the Taj Falaknuma Palace is *the* sensorial treat for you. Set 2,000 feet above Hyderabad, this palace in the sky proudly revels in its splendid historical and geographical setting. The Palace is laid out in a striking scorpion shape and is considered to be the pinnacle of luxury with its exceptional decor. There is a Palace historian who can take you on a personalised guided tour that includes three historical suites, with the main

Palace at the scorpion's head, the guest rooms in its middle, and the dining rooms and Gol Bungalow in the tail. There are shades of empire throughout with lush fabrics, antique furniture and impressively adorned high ceilings, lending a touch of glamour to every suite.

Spending time in the Palace Library may not be an obvious holiday pastime, but this is no ordinary place. Modelled on the library at Windsor Castle, the shelves groan with the weight of some of the rarest

manuscripts from around the world. It is an enlightening experience which is worth the detour for any book lover. Lighter forms of entertainment include the Jiva Spa and yoga room, evening Qawwali devotional singing and music at the Gol Bungalow, the Jade Room, known for its themed high teas, and various restaurants which specialise in great local and world cuisine. To end the day, we particularly love the relaxed atmosphere poolside at the Rotunda, where you can pull up a sun lounger, sip cocktails and watch the world go by.

Top left
Aravali Suites are bright, tasteful and spacious

Bottom left
Modern and classical design merge in a peaceful setting

Above
Bathroom with a spectacular view of the Aravali Hills

DEVI GARH

UDAIPUR, INDIA
COORDINATES: Ⓝ 24° 46' 22.2234" Ⓔ 73° 44' 58.2936"

The 18th-century Devi Garh Palace. near Udaipur in Rajasthan, has been lovingly restored to the all-suite luxury hotel it is today. With a look of modern India, local marbles and semi-precious stones are used to striking effect, set against the heritage of this extraordinary palace in the Aravali Hills. All the hotel's 39 suites are unique.

Bar with its eclectic selection of rare whiskeys and wines, accompanied by an array of mouthwatering snacks, and there is the option of private dining at special venues in the numerous lounges, terraces and gardens. Why not practice yoga and meditation on the ramparts of the palace with only the sound of running water in the

TAJ LAKE PALACE

UDAIPUR, INDIA
COORDINATES: Ⓝ 24° 35' 5.7078" Ⓔ 73° 40' 59.6748"

With the majestic Aravalli Mountains on one side and lofty palaces on the other, the Taj Lake Palace's regal splendour reigns supreme. The most remarkable sight, this palace actually appears to float on the lake at Udaipur and is clearly one of the most enduring symbols of Indian architecture. From the moment you step onto the boat that takes you to the middle of Lake Pichola and the palace, the amazing experience begins. There are some wonderful details – a rose-petal welcome, musicians and dancers at sunset,

the glass of sparkling wine as you're shown around the hotel, lily-filled ponds, alluring fountains and monuments all around.

There's incredible food in store with the Gangaur – The Historic Royal Barge dining experience. Take a night and enjoy an intimate meal on the Royal Gangaur Barge drifting across the water of Lake Pichola. The historic barge of the royal house of Mewar was featured in the James Bond movie, Octopussy. Even today the barge retains its century-old ambience due to its regal decor and the splendour

of its vibrant colours. Seven rowers, in traditional attire, take the guests for the trip of a lifetime around the mystical Lake Pichola. There aren't many places where you get to sample sophisticated cuisine and watch the sunset across the Aravalli Mountains and on the Monsoon Palace, plus a spectacular firework finale.

If you're in search of romance and curious about romantic India, the Taj Lake Palace will remain in your memory for the rest of your life.

Above
The Chandra Prakash (Lustre of the Moon) Suite features decorative gilt and marble

Top right
The luminous Palace Terrace looks out over a mystical Lake Pichola

Bottom right
The Sajjan Niwas Suite bedroom features frescoes of the Krishna Hindu deity

123
124
125
126

INDIA

127
128
129
130

Top left
Terrace Haveli Suites
offer spacious luxury
accommodation

Bottom left
Pool Pavilions have a
private swimming pool
in a peaceful garden

Above
A rooftop pavilion is a
shaded sanctuary with
breathtaking views

AMANBAGH

AJABGARH, INDIA
COORDINATES: Ⓝ 27° 10' 9.1014" Ⓔ 76° 17' 40.1964"

A getaway to the award-winning
Amanbagh, nestled in the Aravalli
Hills, is the ultimate hotel experience.
Steeped in history, culture and beauty,
the palatial building is a window onto
the rich heritage of Rajasthan in all its
splendour. Staying in the Pool Pavilion
is a slice of personal heaven with an
entrance foyer twinkling with lights
that leads you directly to your own
emerald-green marble pool, a gorgeous
bedroom on one side and a spacious,
domed bathroom on the other.

If you can drag yourself away, you could
hop on a bike or take a camel, horse or
jeep ride for an adventure to ancient
Somsagar Lake or a trip to explore the
"haunted" ruins at Bhangarh.
The only fitting end to such a
memorable day would be at the Spa
at the heart of the hotel resort. It's a
large open oasis with a heated outdoor
wading pool and overhanging palm
trees. Where better to start those yoga
and meditation sessions you've been
promising yourself for years?

ANANDA IN THE HIMALAYAS

UTTARAKHAND, INDIA
COORDINATES: Ⓝ 30° 9' 28.4256" Ⓔ 78° 17' 30.4146"

India is the birthplace of the ancient arts of yoga, meditation and Ayurveda, making the Ananda in the Himalayas a great starting point for a holistic life. Flawless staff and service have rightfully earned this luxury spa its multiple industry awards. Where else can you kick-start the day with a yoga session that boasts the Himalayas as a backdrop? It's hard to believe you're only an hour's flight from New Delhi. Spend your day enjoying the personalised spa treatments like the detox, weight loss and Ayurvedic rejuvenation programmes. The serene surroundings overlooking the Rishikesh Valley make even the most arduous hill trek seem enjoyable. The exquisite meals contain the finest organic produce, after which you can retreat to your room where your evening bath has been run. In this tranquil environment the focus is you and the team ensures you escape the stresses of daily life. Something you surely deserve.

123
124
125
126
127

INDIA

128
129
130

Above
The Music Pavilion is a tranquil setting for yoga classes

Top right
The Viceregal Suite is situated in the precincts of the Maharaja's Palace

Bottom right
Villas, set in the Himalayan foothills, feature private swimming pools

Top left
Bedrooms offer comfort within a unique exploration of nomadic tents

Bottom left
A pavilion extends from each tent into a private garden and valley beyond

Above
Bathrooms have all the facilities expected of luxury hotel accommodation

RASA RESORTS

RAJASTHAN, INDIA
COORDINATES: Ⓝ 26° 59' 23.8266" Ⓔ 75° 51' 48.7764"

If you like the idea of mixing luxury with adventure, then Rasa Resort will tick all your boxes. Beyond the walls of Jaipur's Amer Fort lies a magical tented hotel complex, nestled in a

like grid of outdoor textures. The extraordinary effect is that you see the land as a living sculpture changing with the seasons.

DEVI RATN

JAIPUR, INDIA
COORDINATES: (N) 26° 54' 58.6332" (E) 75° 52' 48.9036"

Devi Ratn in Jaipur is a sparkling new jewel in Devi Resorts' crown. Taking its name from Nav Ratn – meaning nine pure, celestial gemstones – this extraordinary location lives up to its name. Jaipur's lustrous gem craft is used to stunning effect in the lyrical spaces and bold architecture of this boutique hotel. The attention to detail can be seen in every stone and pattern in the suites, villas and public spaces, such as the bar and poolside restaurant where etchings reflect the blue water. The celestial ambience flows to The Devi Spa by L'Occitane – a luxurious escape from the city. If you only indulge once during your stay, sample the French beauty brand's wonderful products, and the unique combination of Indian and Mediterranean treatments.

Above
Contemporary Indian and European cuisine is served in a traditional setting

Top right
All 63 Suites at Devi Ratn are celebrations of textures, patterns and colour

Bottom right
Bathrooms have a black river stone finish with a white marble sunken bath

123
124
125
126
127
128
129
130

INDIA

123
124
125
126
127
128
129
130

INDIA

Top left
Relax in the luxury of the Rajput Suite living area

Bottom left
Pamper yourself in style in the Dutch Suite bathroom

Above
Poolside: a reflection of architectural brilliance

THE TAJ MAHAL PALACE

MUMBAI, INDIA
COORDINATES: (N) 18° 55' 17.7204" (E) 72° 50' 0.2328"

A stay at The Taj Mahal Palace is an extraordinary way to discover Mumbai. Its location offers sweeping panoramic views of the Gateway to India and the Arabian Sea. The hotel itself is a visual treat – a breathtaking feat of architecture and a brilliant combination of Moorish, Oriental and Florentine styles. The friendly staff go to great pains to ensure that guests experience authenticity and luxury with carefully organised tours, events and dining experiences to cater for any number of tastes.

There are two sections of the hotel, the Tower and the Palace. The walk that leads to the Palace suites is extraordinary. The corridors leading to your room are lined with genuine artefacts and antiques that are testimony to a rich Indian heritage of which this hotel is rightfully proud. You'll be greeted with garlands and special butler service.

The state-of-the-art suites are decked out in three parts, including a sumptuous and enormous en-suite marble bathroom with hydro-massage hand shower, the only way to relax and retreat from the hectic flurry of Mumbai's colourful streets. Highlights at the hotel are the Chef Studio, offering an unparalleled gourmet dining experience, and the fabulous Golden Dragon restaurant where you must be sure to sample the chef's speciality dish, Song of the Dragon. Ask the friendly staff about the Heritage Walk where you are taken on a guided tour that explains Indian history, art and architecture, ending with a flourish and champagne in the exclusive Palace Lounge. A trip fit for a king and his queen.

THE STRAND YANGON

YANGON, MYANMAR
COORDINATES: (N) 16° 46' 9.3072" (E) 96° 9' 45.3312"

Stepping into The Strand sweeps you back in time to an era of colonial grandeur when guests sip legendary Strand Sours in the bar, as large fans revolve energetically from high ceilings. Located in the heart of Yangon, the hotel is a three-storey, Victorian-style property, which is brimming with charm and lives up to its reputation as one of the finest hotels in the city. All suites are serviced by a team of butlers, providing 24-hour service with discreet professionalism. The rooms epitomise timeless elegance, boasting high ceilings, teak floors, and a spacious living area to relax in. The sumptuous Strand Grill is renowned for innovative culinary creations, while The Strand Café serves delicious Western and Burmese specialties throughout the day. And, after experiencing the buzz of the city, complete your stay with a relaxing massage in the hotel spa.

Above
At the centre of the hotel, the lobby is grand but comfortable and welcoming

Top right
The Strand is a beautifully renovated stately landmark with old-world charm

Bottom right
All suites are tastefully furnished with comfort and luxury in mind

TRISARA

PHUKET, THAILAND
COORDINATES: (N) 8° 2' 9.7944" (E) 98° 16' 33.5382"

Hidden among the lush, tropical jungle of a private bay, one of South-East Asia's most intimate and exclusive getaways offers a true sense of privacy. Scott Manson travelled to Thailand's "Third Garden in Heaven"

A long plane journey gives you a great perspective on the world, in the same way a good Martini does or a lungful of smoke from a prize Cohiba cigar. This rare pause to reflect during my flight from London to Phuket provided time to consider the fabulous options available to me on this Thai odyssey. From cookery classes and Thai boxing instruction to luxury boat trips, I wanted to cram as many experiences as I could into just a few days. Next to me, a couple of gap-year types chattered away about their three-month plan for seeing Thailand and I couldn't help but feel envious of their extended stay. Those endless, carefree days of my youth felt so long away. Then I heard them discussing how they wouldn't be able to afford the extra 50p per day per room for their own toilet. Suddenly, age, guile and a couple of credit cards looked a far better deal than youth, irresponsibility and a bad haircut.

I left them outside the airport, haggling over a taxi fare, while I slipped into an air-conditioned 4x4, which whisked me off to my tropical paradise. Trisara is a handsome boutique

property, situated north of the busy coastal tourist zone of Phuket, in the area of Nai Thon beach. And while it's a convenient 15-minute transfer from the airport, the 40-minute drive to Phuket ensures that the majority of its residents are here to relax, as opposed to hitting the town's notorious all-night Patong area until the early hours. Indeed, a sense of peace pervades the entire resort – Trisara in Sanskrit means Third Garden in Heaven – and the only sound to be heard is the chatter of birds and the whisper of wind through the many palm trees. As I gazed out at the setting sun, casting fiery flickers over my villa's private ten-metre infinity pool, I felt the rigours of a 20-hour journey slip away.

Now, everyone has a rigid standard operating procedure when it comes to first entering a hotel room or villa, and I am no different. Shoes off, jump on bed, establish comfiness (very high), check out bathroom (clean, contemporary, lots of fluffy towels, ridiculously large bath, indoor and outdoor shower), sip complimentary drink (lemongrass and ginger tea), while lolling about on the bed, flicking

through the TV channels and reading the hotel's welcome-pack guide (great food recommendations + no spelling mistakes = winner).

Wandering onto the teak sundeck, with its stunning view of the Andaman Sea, I'm struck by the sheer level of privacy that a Trisara Pool Villa provides. Although there are villas to my left and right, they cannot see me, and I can't see them. Even the hotel staff have to use a doorbell and then come in to the property by a side entrance, so that they cause as little disturbance as possible. Very handy if you're the type who likes to take a dip "au naturel".

Dinner that night was taken on the expansive outdoor deck, surrounded by lazily swaying coconut palms. Service was whip smart, but understated. There was none of that "hushed temple of gastronomy" nonsense – the place was high-end and offered fine dining, for sure, but relaxed enough that you could happily put your elbows on the table or drop a fork on the floor without fear of the whole place staring at you in silent reproach. Prawns, chicken and the shredded red buds of the banana tree, among other things, went into my dinner, but its brilliance, as with all the best Thai dishes, lay in the complexity of its seasonings – sour in the front of the mouth (tamarind pulp), fiery in the back (dried chilies) and sweetly nutty at the top (coconut cream). Eating it left me reeling with pleasure.

There was also wonderful Tom Kha Gai, that vibrant chicken soup. Hot, rich and sharp, it owed everything to the liltingly fresh, vividly perfumed lemon grass, holy basil, coriander, coconut milk and kaffir lime leaves that flavored it, along with the obligatory chili. A contended burp – pardon me – and a coffee signalled to the staff that I was ready to hit the hay. The next day, after eating some of the finest pain au chocolate I've had outside Paris, courtesy of Trisara's in-house bakery, I decided to find a local Thai boxing gym and do a little training. I got there at 7am and stood around nervously sipping water, stretching and watching the other pupils arrive. When one particularly fierce-looking chap turned up, all tattoos, muscles, short and squat – like an attack hamster – I sing-sang under my breath "Oh God, I'm dead". The Aussie pupil next to me glanced up and then moved away. No one wants to stand next to the weedy bloke in the class.

The gym was as spartan as Russ's conversation. Just a ring, some weight machines, lots of punch bags and a roof. The sides were open, allowing muggy air to circulate and passers-by to look in on the action.

Still, at least I could drag my aching body back to a beautiful hotel, as opposed to the small wooden huts next to the gym, where most of the fighters stayed.

While my fellow fighters wrestled with damp sheets and weak overhead fans, I could lie back on Egyptian cotton, watching movies on widescreen TV and pumping the air con up to US-shopping-mall levels of chill.

"I feel a bit guilty," I said in a Skype call home to my wife. "But only a bit." My reasoning was that, actually, I had it far tougher than those living at the Muay Thai camp in their wooden huts. They were roused from their beds at 6am by a bloke banging a gong. I had to get myself up and motivated enough to skip Trisara's excellent breakfast options – offering everything from faultless full English to Thai curry – and drive my sorry self down to the gym. I was the one with the willpower. Those tattooed pro fighters had it easy. The next morning saw me skip the boxing to take one of the hotel's Thai cookery classes. Held in the resort's vast kitchens and run by an incredibly patient Thai chef, I was schooled in the art of creating a sweet-and-sour prawn soup, Thai green curry and, my personal favourite, Pad Thai. The fact that I then had to sit down and eat all of this for my lunch, meant that any energetic activity was also off the menu for the rest of the afternoon. Instead, the super-efficient reception team organised a last-minute boat trip for me to the James Bond island, known locally as Ko Tapu, a stunning spot made famous in the 1974 film *The Man With The Golden Gun*.

There are lots of mysterious things about boats, such as why anyone would get on one voluntarily. It all seems like terrifically hard work. Head to any marina at the weekend and you'll see hordes of amusement-seekers setting up folding chairs and spending an afternoon watching boat owners perform comical maneuvers, such as forgetting to put their handbrake on and seeing their car roll down the ramp into the sea. Any honest boat owner would agree that putting your boat into the water is definitely asking for trouble. Most have had their boats sitting on their driveways long enough for them to be registered historical landmarks. Given my clear misgivings about all things sea-faring, the knowledge that there would be a Trisara-supplied lunch on a far-flung beach, with a view of some of the world's most impressive stalactites and stalagmites, helped clinch it for me. This was probably one of the best decisions I have ever made. It's a truly breathtaking area so, if anyone asks you whether you'd like to take a boat trip to Phang Nga, "yes" is the only appropriate answer. Oh, and if there's a better feeling than sipping on a chilled Chablis while eating a lobster, bacon and avocado club sandwich on a deserted beach, as your personal motor launch bobs about in the turquoise sea, then I've yet to experience it.

In a decade of hotel reviewing, the one question people always ask me is "Where's the best place you've stayed?" I've always fudged the answer a bit, mentioning two or three lovely spots. Trisara has given me the definitive answer. Seriously, it's that good. Stay here.

132
133
134
135
136
137
138

THAILAND

Top left
Two Bedroom Ocean Front Pool Villa

Bottom left
Ocean View Pool Villas combine breathtaking views with complete privacy

Top
A view of luxury and total relaxation from your private infinity pool

THAILAND

132
133
134

135
136
137
138

Top left
WOW Ocean Haven with private sun deck and pool

Bottom left
TONIC BAR serves wellness in a glass plus healthy snacks

Above
W LOUNGE features chic lotus-shaped sunken seats

W RETREAT KOH SAMUI

KOH SAMUI, THAILAND
COORDINATES: Ⓝ 9° 34' 22.296" Ⓔ 100° 0' 59.7018"

Chic, hip and stylish, W Retreat Koh Samui is nothing short of glamorous. Attention to detail is something that W does so well – the scented cold towels on arrival after your long-haul flight, the Munchie Box in your villa that's stocked with snacks for those midnight cravings, the Sweet Spot full of complimentary ice cream and cold drinks perfect for those hot afternoons, a turn-down treat every evening, think popcorn and cookies. There's even cool music drifting into the public areas to add to the calm and funky ambiance.

You'll arrive with grand plans to explore the island of Koh Samui. However, after a couple of days, the lure of your private sun deck and pool, the uber-comfortable sun loungers on the beach, the unique Thaimazcal® spa experience (don't leave without trying this) and the amazing sunsets from SIP bar – and that's just a handful of WOW factors – are enough to keep you Retreat-based and happy.

INTERCONTINENTAL SAMUI BAAN TALING NGAM RESORT

KOH SAMUI, THAILAND
COORDINATES: Ⓝ 9° 27' 46.5876" Ⓔ 99° 56' 5.337"

Over the past ten years, Koh Samui has been transformed from a sleepy backpacker town into a vibrant and hip destination. But it's not all about raucous full-moon parties – if these aren't really your thing, then experience the powder-soft beaches, fresh seafood, friendly locals and unpretentious vibe. As the first luxury hotel to open on the island, the InterContinental Samui Baan Taling Ngam Resort secured an enviable location on the quieter west coast. It is set in 22 acres of tropical gardens and coconut trees, cascading down a hillside onto a white sandy beach – truly idyllic.

If you like beach holidays, but quickly get bored of sunbathing, then this resort is for you. There are enough water sports and land-based activities to keep you occupied during a weeks' stay. If you want to explore the local surroundings, then the concierge is on hand to guide you. The resort also has a private pier and is an ideal base for island hopping.

But if this all sounds a little too energetic, then simply gaze at the ocean views from the comfort of your hillside suite, drift from your beachfront Pool Villa for a dip in the sea, relax by one of the seven outdoor swimming pools – you'll never struggle to find an available sun lounger – or try a treatment in the spa, or even on the beach – the Thai massage is heavenly. Your most difficult daily decision will be which of the specially concocted cocktails to choose as you watch the spectacular sunset from the cliffside Air Bar.

132
133
134
135
THAILAND
136
137
138

 Above
An Ocean View Suite bathroom combines luxury and style

Top right
The resort is located within the exclusive enclave of Taling Ngam

Bottom right
A Tropical Pavilion bedroom offers comfort and convenience

THAILAND

132
133
134
135
136
137
138

Top left
Front Lobby: a seamless blend of nature and the built environment

Bottom left
Junior Pool Suites have a private pool and Jacuzzi, plus sea views

Above
Grand Pool Suites feature private infinity swimming pools

THE RACHA

PHUKET, THAILAND
COORDINATES: Ⓝ 7° 48' 15.789" Ⓔ 98° 20' 17.2572"

You know you're in for a divine experience the moment you set foot in The Racha Resort. Our welcoming staff at reception set the tone but, as you sip your drink and select the perfect scent for your room, nothing prepares you for what's to come. Trust us – it will take some willpower to drag yourself from your luxurious villa and private pool, if you choose a pool suite. And when you do, it'll be worth it.

If it's tension you need to rid yourself of, the yoga sessions are remarkable and the Anumba Spa is well worth a visit, particularly if you sample the Signature Package or the Thai Flower Ritual treatment.

There are a wide range of dining choices and we take particular pride in preparing local delicacies. In our book, the barbequed seafood is a winner. It's the most mouthwatering dish of the holiday.

Be sure to take in the natural beauty that defines the island from the crystal-clear turquoise waters to the pristine white beaches, perfect for snorkelling and other fun-filled water activities. It's your opportunity to experience deluxe, environmentally sustainable tourism.

PARESA RESORT

PHUKET, THAILAND
COORDINATES: Ⓝ 7° 55' 57.12" Ⓔ 98° 15' 44.92"

You'll be forgiven for thinking you've landed in heaven as you arrive at Paresa Resort in Phuket. In fact, Paresa translated means heaven of all heavens and the name is certainly no exaggeration. An accommodating team of angels – Paresa's concierge staff – go out of their way to ensure your stay is as blissful as possible, from a fresh bowl of fruit waiting for you upon arrival, to a selection of tasty canapes brought to your room every evening.

Sitting atop the cliffs of Kamala, Paresa blends harmoniously with its tropical surroundings. It's built around magnificent banyan trees that provide natural shade for the alfresco restaurant and glorious infinity pool. Sitting under their leafy canopies, you can really soak up the tranquillity of this paradise. Each of Paresa's open-plan villas overlooks the Andaman Sea and, if you're lucky enough to stay in the top-floor Cielo Residence, you'll experience truly breathtaking views. Huge bath tubs, luxury bed linen and private plunge pools complete this picture of utter luxury.

Paresa's cookery school hosts daily classes, where you can learn how to make classic Thai dishes with fresh ingredients bought from the local market. But if your culinary skills aren't up to scratch, Paresa's amazing Thai and Italian restaurants will provide so many options to satisfy your gastronomic needs. For a romantic experience you'll never forget, dine on a "private island" in the beautifully lit infinity pool. You'll feel like you're floating in a star-lit sky.

132
133
134
135
136
137
138

Above
Cielo Residence is the ultimate Phuket luxury pool villa

Top right
The Aqua Suite offers a sensual pool villa experience

Bottom right
Dima tub: relax in a bath of scented flower petals

132
133
134
135
136
137
138

THAILAND

Top left
The outdoor Swimming Pool is bordered by a relaxing sun terrace

Bottom left
The Restaurant building once housed the British Consulate

Above
Ten private Spa Suites have steam showers and terrazzo bathtubs

THE CHEDI CHIANG MAI

CHIANG MAI, THAILAND
COORDINATES: Ⓝ 18° 46' 54.3432" Ⓔ 99° 0' 12.9954"

Behind architect Kerry Hill's four-storey bamboo-clad wall lies one of Thailand's most striking modern buildings, the only riverside five-star hotel in Chiang Mai. The Chedi Chiang Mai, located along the scenic Mae Ping River, is designed to blend into its natural surroundings with carefully planned landscaping.

Floor-to-ceiling sliding glass doors feature in all 84 of the sleek guest rooms, looking out onto the traditional fishing boats floating past. Lingering on a river-facing balcony or by the pool in this oasis of calm, it's hard to believe that you're

right in the heart of Chiang Mai. The Spa at The Chedi is widely regarded as one of the best in the world, and it's easy to see why with its heavenly setting, REN product treatments and sophisticated amenities. Wile away the afternoon with a delicious mojito signature cocktail or take afternoon tea, something of an institution with local residents in the Colonial House. This remarkable building used to house the British Consulate and is now an exclusive restaurant serving the finest Thai, Indian and Western cuisine.

If you can drag yourself away, do take the time to step outside and discover what this country has to offer. Top of your must-see list should be northern Thailand's wonderful elephants, easily the region's most famous attraction. Take a day trek through the lush countryside and see them in their natural habitat. There are fabulous Buddhist temples to explore and the famed night bazaar, near Chiang Mai's old town, is shopping heaven, just a short walk from the hotel.

THE NAM HAI HOI AN

HOI AN, VIETNAM
COORDINATES: (N) 15° 52′ 46.704″ (E) 108° 19′ 54.2634″

Nestled in 35 hectares of gorgeously landscaped gardens, fronting a mile-long white sandy beach, The Nam Hai is a haven of calm after the bustle of Hoi An town.

Staying in one of the stunning Pool Villas is like stepping into a mini oasis. You'll be spoilt for choice with a private infinity pool and direct access to the beach. Your individual butler serves afternoon tea and mixes complimentary cocktails before a gourmet dinner at one of the resort's Vietnamese or international restaurants. Back in your room, there'll be candles and soft music to complement luxurious beds and sunken bathtubs.

The Nam Hai is also close to the three UNESCO World Heritage Sites of Hoi An, My Son Sanctuary and the Imperial City of Hue. With plenty of activities to enjoy though – cooking classes, tennis and a heavenly floating spa – it's likely you won't leave the resort.

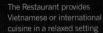

Above
The Restaurant provides Vietnamese or international cuisine in a relaxed setting

Top right
Nam Hai Villas are elegantly furnished and well-equipped

Bottom right
The Beach Restaurant offers gourmet alfresco dining

Top left
The Beach Club features an open-air pavilion and shaded deck

Bottom left
Amanpulo's impressive 30-metre swimming pool, pictured at night

Above
Bordered by clear blue waters, Amanpulo is an island paradise

AMANPULO

PAMALICAN ISLAND, PHILIPPINES
COORDINATES: Ⓝ 11° 18' 58.3776" Ⓔ 120° 40' 59.7216"

As you touch down at Manila Airport, you know you're in for a luxurious time – your private plane awaits to take you to Pamalican Island and to the heaven that is Amanpulo. This resort has its own airstrip and is surrounded by turquoise waters, coral reefs and endless white sands. It's all here – windsurfing, scuba diving and snorkelling for action-packed days and wonderful massage treatments at the spa for lazy evenings.

This luxury resort comprises a series of casitas, each with its own beach area. Every detail is taken care of by a team of dedicated staff who weave in and out of sight with the utmost discretion. There are many ways to dine – alfresco, tucking into sea food or barbecue grills at the Beach Club, oven-fired pizzas at the Windsurf Hut-Picnic Grove, or Vietnamese specialities at the Lagoon Club. The perfect end to a day of perfect rest and

BUNGA RAYA ISLAND RESORT & SPA

KOTA KINABALU, MALAYSIA
COORDINATES: Ⓝ 6° 0' 46.6806" Ⓔ 116° 2' 53.628"

Bunga Raya Island Resort & Spa, situated on the island of Gaya and part of Sabah in Malaysian Borneo, is an extraordinary property which works in synergy with nature.

The resort is sumptuous and prides itself on its Marine Ecology Research Centre (MERC), which aims to preserve the marine environment. Nature is a serious business here, and guests can play their part in the restoration and protection of the resort through MERC's Adopt-a-Coral programme. The original forest, enveloping the resort, is protected throughout with trees left untouched or ingeniously integrated into the decor.

Bunga Raya Island Resort & Spa has 48 hillside villas, 11 with direct access to the beach. For a regal experience, the Royal Villa takes the prize, backed by tropical jungle on one side and the South China Sea on the other. A private arrival jetty leads to an elegant building constructed of tropical hardwood. A designated butler, chef and housekeeper will be at your service around the clock. The villa has several classy dining areas, as well as comfortable living rooms and a full-size designer kitchen. All you have to do is decide where to relax – on the spacious outdoor deck, complete with its two private plunge pools, on your own private beach, or at the luxurious spa with its menu of indulgent treatments. This luxurious experience and the attention to detail brought to guests by the obliging staff will restore your faith in how we can celebrate nature's beauty with intelligence and sensitivity.

Above
The Koi Restaurant offers fresh local cuisine with mouthwatering views

Top right
View from the Hilltop Villa, the highest point of the property

Bottom right
Villas, built from natural materials, have private pools and magnificent views

Top left
The hotel blends rich heritage with contemporary style

Bottom left
Town Restaurant overlooks the charming Singapore River

Above
The Governor Suite opens out onto a magnificent verandah

THE FULLERTON HOTEL SINGAPORE

SINGAPORE
COORDINATES: Ⓝ 1° 17' 10.2834" Ⓔ 103° 51' 10.6812"

As you arrive at The Fullerton Hotel, you can't help but be awestruck by its magnificence.

Once home to the nation's General Post Office, the Chamber of Commerce and the exclusive Singapore Club, this striking building is now one of the most prestigious hotels in the city. The aim is to make every guest feel as special as the Club's elite members who visited before you. The hotel's arresting facade, complete with classical columns and elaborate portes-cochères, evokes memories

The decor is fresh and contemporary; the staff are friendly and highly professional. With eleven different styles of room – from the spacious Quay Rooms, overlooking the Singapore River, to the exquisite two-storey Loft Suites, with a private balcony – you are guaranteed a uniquely luxurious experience, whichever you choose.

Despite being within walking distance of Singapore's cultural and entertainment hotspots, there's so much to do in the hotel you'll never

with a delicious homemade cake from the Cake Boutique, relax in the heavenly Asian Spa or explore the Heritage Gallery, a showcase of the hotel's legacy through photographs. Gastronomes will be thrilled to discover the incredible variety of cuisine on offer – Italian, Japanese and Indian, to name but a few. Moreover, if you're lucky enough to be staying in a Suite, there are extra surprises in store at The Straits Club with a daily champagne breakfast, afternoon tea, and evening cocktails and canapes.

THE FULLERTON BAY HOTEL SINGAPORE

SINGAPORE
COORDINATES: (N) 1°16' 59.343" (E) 103° 51' 9.8418"

The Fullerton Bay Hotel Singapore made a splash at its opening in 2010 as the only hotel on the waters of Marina Bay, the city's latest destination for business and leisure that bristles with action. The hotel cuts a dashing figure with dazzling exteriors and glamorous interiors, and deserves the accolades received from Condé Nast Traveller magazine which named it as one of the world's top new hotels, Travel + Leisure which featured it in the coveted It List 2011, and Business Traveller which recognised The Fullerton Bay Hotel as one of the best business hotels in the world.

There are just 100 guest rooms and suites here which makes for an intimate, relaxed ambience and one which calms the soul as you step through the doors. This is the perfect place to take time out from Singapore's bustling city life and slip into the lap of luxury. Floor-to-ceiling windows in every spacious room afford sweeping views of the Marina Bay waterfront and Singapore's glittering skyline. Decor in rooms and suites echoes the beauty of the panoramic views outside. Details are fashioned from the finest rosewood, ivory limestone and marble, and in the bathrooms

the luxury toiletries come courtesy of Molton Brown Hotel Therapies. Guests want for nothing with an in-room Nespresso machine, a well-stocked minibar, fine Egyptian cotton linen and complimentary wi-fi access throughout the hotel. Don't miss Lantern, the stylish rooftop bar that's been dubbed one of the best hotel bars by CNN's travel website CNNGO. Bedecked with vintage-inspired furniture, including romantic daybeds, it's set in a lush tropical environment, reflecting the beauty of Singapore.

Above
The Lobby is a statement of contemporary luxury and refined elegance

Top right
Premier Bay View Rooms have vistas of the Marina Bay waterfront

Bottom right
The hotel boasts spectacular views of the bay and Singapore skyline

Top left
The Presidential Suite on the 20th floor is the pinnacle of luxury

Bottom left
The Remède Spa offers customised treatments to suit individual needs

Above
Glamorous French marble bathroom of an Executive Deluxe Room

THE ST. REGIS SINGAPORE

SINGAPORE
COORDINATES: (N) 1° 18' 21.996" (E) 103° 49' 34.2516"

Arriving in the heart of Singapore and checking into the St. Regis Singapore is a refined affair. This exceptionally elegant hotel boasts the only butler service in the city that caters for every guest – your luggage is taken care of and unpacked, your shoes polished, there are round-the-clock refreshments – leaving you to enjoy the fun. A good kick-start for weary limbs is a visit to the Remède Spa that offers luxurious signature treatments, like the soothing, warm jade-stone massage for total rejuvenation. Be sure to try the fabulous new Mani:Pedi:Cure Studio by Bastien Gonzalez that pampers with its revolutionary approach to hand and foot care. Wine lovers are in for a treat with a daily wine and cheese appreciation at Decanter's elite tasting bar, including more than 800 global labels to complement your favourite cuisine, be it French, Italian or Cantonese. With all this, you're guaranteed a perfect stay at one of the world's most sumptuous and sophisticated addresses.

BANYAN TREE BINTAN

BINTAN, INDONESIA
COORDINATES: Ⓝ 1° 11' 5.0676" Ⓔ 104° 20' 32.2692"

Banyan Tree Bintan is an extraordinary resort. It overlooks the South China Sea with views that are arresting, offering a hint of what's still to come at this all-villa resort. It's hard to believe that this idyllic hideaway is only a 45 minute ferry ride from the hustle and bustle of Singapore. Every last luxurious detail instils a sense of serenity and calm that's greatly valued by the discerning clientele who come here to escape.

Local resources are plentiful, and the menus are varied and deliciously fresh with seafood, meats and salads prepared by talented chefs. If you prefer a quiet, intimate dinner, opt for a sumptuous in-villa barbeque or choose one of the unique Destination Dining experiences for two on the beach, by the pool or high above the rocks, the waves crashing below. The villas are varied in their layout and configuration, and all offer huge living areas with polished decor, sunken baths, as well as private jet or infinity pools surrounded by tropical forest and plenty of outdoor space for relaxing under the sun or stars. Explore the stunning natural environment and plan a fishing trip, speedboat ride or water-skiing adventure around the island. If rest and relaxation are more your thing, the Banyan Tree Spa specialises in heavenly Eastern therapies to wile away the hours in this heavenly place. Golf enthusiasts are spoilt with the 18-hole Laguna Bintan Golf Club designed by Greg Norman. The stunning course runs through 60 hectares of lush landscape winding through forest, wetlands and beachfront coconut groves.

Above
Destination Dining for an intimate outdoor culinary experience

Top right
The Bayfront Pool Villa offers luxury with an awe-inspiring view

Bottom right
The Banyan Tree Spa Bintan is a sanctuary for the senses

INDONESIA

Top left
The sun sets over the hotel's infinity pool and the Indian Ocean

Bottom left
The Club at The Legian offers exclusive villa accommodation

Above
The three-bedroom Beach House is ideal for a family getaway

THE LEGIAN BALI

BALI, INDONESIA
COORDINATES: Ⓢ 8° 41' 4.0626" Ⓔ 115° 9' 13.1214"

There are few places in the world that can beat the stunning beachfront sunset at The Legian Bali on Seminyak Beach. The suites bring a touch of home-from-home luxury with sumptuous four-poster beds, spacious bathrooms, elegant and modern furnishings, and facilities that make it difficult to leave your room. You will venture out, however, to take a dip in the nearby pristine pool before indulging in a heavenly Balinese massage at the spa. Dinner at the hotel is not to be missed with delicious menus from around the world and well-selected wines available. Staff will go to great lengths to ensure your every need is fulfilled, be it a regular supply of chilled water or sun cream, and you can indulge in complimentary afternoon tea every day. For the ultimate getaway to an authentic setting, you could not do better than this dream destination.

W RETREAT & SPA BALI-SEMINYAK

BALI, INDONESIA
COORDINATES: (S) 8° 40' 38.013" (E) 115° 9' 1.065"

W Retreat & Spa Bali – Seminyak opened in March 2011 and has already made an impression on the Island of the Gods. Contemporary and cutting-edge, with a fun, relaxed vibe, this uber-chic retreat is Bali's trendiest enclave. Vibrantly designed with the latest mod cons, luxurious and comfortable, the retreats and villas are private sanctuaries that you will never want to leave – and you actually don't have to. It is, however, worth dragging yourself out of your ultra-comfortable W signature bed for a breakfast experience – an endless feast of delights, from fresh tropical juices to gourmet coffees, pastries to pancakes, eggs of your liking to cold meat and cheeses, and that's not even starting on the sushi and sashimi.

After such a hearty start to the day, you'll probably fancy a doze on a day bed by the tropical-feel pool. You need never move from this spot all day as the friendly W team are on hand to ensure you don't have to lift a finger, regularly supplying snacks (more food) and sun cream.

There's a gym if you really feel the need to burn off some of those breakfast calories, but holidays are all about relaxing and indulgence, so allow yourself a treatment at the 24-hour AWAY Spa instead, (yes, you can get a massage at midnight).

As you would expect from a W Retreat, the evening vibe is fun and funky. Mingle over a Martini at sunset, against a sound backdrop of DJ beats, before cosying up at Starfish Bloo in a "fishtrap" booth (when you see it, you'll understand) – and don't miss the Japanese hot rocks.

Above
Starfish Bloo serves pan-Asian cuisine in a casual but stylish beachside setting

Top right
A Marvellous One-Bedroom Pool Villa comes with 24-hour valet service

Bottom right
The WET pool is inspired by Indonesian rice fields and overlooks the beach

145
146
147
148

INDONESIA

Top left
The Restaurant and Club Lounge is a unique venue for traditional cuisine

Bottom left
Each of the resort's One-Bedroom Suites features a spacious bedroom

Above
Pool Villas each have a ten-metre swimming pool plus sun deck

THE CHEDI CLUB TANAH GAJAH UBUD

BALI, INDONESIA
COORDINATES: Ⓢ 8° 30' 16.365" Ⓔ 115° 16' 1.1892"

As you enjoy breakfast gazing out at the vista of endless rice fields, listening to the wooden wind chimes, you'll feel a true sense of place and a calm spirituality enveloping you that is the essence of Bali.

Set just outside Ubud, The Chedi Club Tanah Gajah is an exclusive boutique property – just 20 suites and villas – boasting a breathtaking rural setting and an ambience of total serenity. The staff are genuinely friendly – your personal butler will assist with any whim – and the complimentary extras, such as the delicious afternoon tea and early-evening cocktails and canapes, are welcome luxuries.

If you want to wow that special person, then you can't beat a private dinner served on the edge of the paddy fields, lit by candles and fireflies. All in all, it's no surprise that The Chedi Club regularly tops the Ubud hotel rankings on Trip Advisor.

AMAN AT SUMMER PALACE

BEIJING, CHINA
COORDINATES: Ⓝ 39° 59' 57.753" Ⓔ 116° 16' 57.2874"

Escape Beijing's pulsating nerve centre in less than 40 minutes and head to Aman at Summer Palace. With a respectful nod to tradition, this luxury hotel is housed in a series of pavilions surrounded by lush gardens and pathways. The original complex once housed imperial guests at the turn of the 20th century and today guests have privileged access to the nearby Summer Palace which is a UNESCO World Heritage Site. Tranquillity is the key here with round-the-clock, expert discretion. Be sure to reward yourself after an afternoon of cultural sightseeing in the hotel spa with a traditional massage and visit the amazing indoor pool. Warm evenings should be spent at the bar by the lotus pond before deciding where to eat. The only worry you'll have all holiday is where to go first?

CHINA

151
152
153
154
155
156
157

Above
Chef Naoki Okumura serves French-Japanese kaiseki fare

Top right
The Spa has nine self-contained double treatment suites

Bottom right
Relax on a reclining daybed by the 25-metre indoor pool

CHINA WORLD SUMMIT WING

BEIJING, CHINA
COORDINATES: (N) 39° 54' 33.9768" (E) 116° 26' 24.9786"

Situated at the top of the China World Trade Centre, an exciting new hotel experience offers discerning guests the opportunity to discover Beijing in style. Nick Clarke sampled the high life

Rise and shine, Beijing – there's a new kid on the block and as any sharp-suited businessman or designer-label lady of leisure will tell you, the kid's worth checking out and checking into. Every sleek, Asian-inspired inch deserves exploration and all from the head-spinning top of the China World Trade Centre. Enter China World Summit Wing, Beijing, managed by Shangri-La, which has five sister properties in the city. Towering above China's hectic capital like an all-seeing eye, you can certainly observe most of Beijing's goings-on from the floor-to-ceiling windows. There are 278 rooms, a host of restaurants, bars and lounges, a stunning gym, spa and pools, where shimmering waters seem to flow forever before cascading over the side of the building and seemingly onto the street below.

Pinging up in the lift, which is fitted with a dazzling crystal chandelier, guests are met by a warm, hospitable staff in a luxe lobby – named the Resident's Foyer – on level 64, dedicated exclusively to those staying at the hotel. You need a key card to access the lobby, other rooms and any area not open to the public. The emphasis here is on relaxing on stylish sofas and armchairs, and enjoying a table laden with every kind of tea, coffee, mineral water, soft drink and snack you could hanker for, after touching down on the tarmac. There's also a bookshelf stocked with highly covetable design tomes, from Taschen to Phaidon, for the thumbing.

With the biggest rooms in Beijing at no less than 55-square-metres, expectations are high when guests are shown along a patterned green hallway and beyond a heavy wooden door. The rooms are grand, gorgeous spaces decked out in warm browns and beiges, interjected with occasional flashes of red, silver and green. It's no wonder the powers that be have thrown shiny golden stars at this hotel. There are king-size beds with fine thread-count sheets, goose-down duvets and pillows so plump they would lull insomniacs into a deep sleep. There are Nespresso machines, bathrooms with sit-down showers, infinity-style bathtubs and generous helpings of L'Occitane toiletries. There are plenty of gadgets for technophiles, such as electric blackout blinds, iPod docking stations, DVD players and flat-screen TVs

built into bathroom mirrors. A large working desk ensures the corporate crowd is looked after too, with complimentary wi-fi and high-end stationery. The unique selling point, however, speaks for itself – the kind of floor-to-ceiling view that has you dropping your bag the moment you walk in. Come haze or crisp blue skies, there's no denying that beyond the glass is a truly breathtaking panorama – a smudged orange watercolour come dusk, a shocking neon-lit sign by night. Beijing Beautiful, they call it.

It's not only the rooms that are unique though. CHI, The Spa has treatment junkies from across the city flocking in their droves for a hit of something holistic. Shangri-La's signature spa brand is given a slightly different spin at this hotel. Gone are the dark and moody Himalayan-inspired interiors of its sister spas, and in its place is a lighter, airier aesthetic that brings the brand right back to its Chinese origins. It's small in comparison to its super-sized siblings, but what it lacks in size, it certainly makes up for in substance. Found on level 77, there are six small but perfectly formed spa suites that contain baths, beds and beautifully appointed private dressing areas. Everything is sultrily lit, while chill-out music creates an ambience to soothe even the most stressed-out office worker. As with all the spas under the Shangri-La umbrella, this one has its signature: the Amber Facial, a scented slice of heaven that has guests' faces pampered for no less than an hour-and-a-half. A quick Q&A prior to treatment matches the facial to the individual, in this case defined by the five elemental signs of earth, fire, water, wood and metal.

When the buffing and beautifying is done, guests head to the health club on level 78 with its treadmills that look out over the city and, for those

tea. As you'd expect, the tea menu is vast, with leaves of all shapes and sizes, to accompany a three-tiered platter of traditional British scones, clotted cream and jam, as well as mini savoury sandwiches. It's all very civilised, served up in a slick, shiny space signposted at the entrance by a sculpture of a tree, branches outstretched, as if welcoming guests into the fold. A sweet spot for afternoon gulping and grazing, there's also heartier fare for lunching. Its views demand contemplation as you sip from a delicate bone-china cup.

There are a number of in-house options when it comes to full-on meals. The hotel's signature restaurant is Grill 79, an opulent space furnished with crisp white-clothed tables, high-backed armchairs, curved booths, chic Murano chandeliers and a palette of vibrant reds, burnt oranges and chocolate browns. The menu is as international as the clientele, and is split into dishes categorised as raw, vegetarian, from the ocean and from the grill. The clue is in the name and diners should sample a special steak. David Blackmore's Wagyu practically melts on your fork and is so rare that the hotel only takes delivery of seven precious slices every month. Those who don't have a head for heights are best off downstairs on level four at Nadaman, an outlet of the high-end Japanese chain. Specialising in kaiseki cuisine – a traditional multi-course dinner – it does for fish what Grill 79 does for meat. Those unfamiliar with kaiseki, something that hasn't yet gained familiarity in the West, should sample the sushi kaiseki lunch option. The focal point of this space is a sculptural tree that rises up from the centre of the dining room, chopstick-shaped branches and twigs climbing across the ceiling. It's a motif that's mirrored on the patterned

perfectly proportioned spaces. The jewel in the hotel's crown is Atmosphere but, despite being the highest bar in Beijing, there's nothing lofty about it. As with other hotel spaces, in particular the wine bar in front of Grill 79, superstar designer Adam Tihany's fingerprint is evident in a turquoise and green glass panel that frames the entrance and two variations of lights that hang inside. Sexy purple armchairs, high leather bar stools, and wine and whisky showcased in room-sized glass boxes, complete the look. Manager Anthony Tschudin certainly knows what he's doing as the drinks are spot-on, with cocktails to suit every guest, occasion and mood, and the bar lays claim to the biggest whisky collection in Beijing. Anthony gives his staff free rein to experiment, using regulars as a tasting panel for innovative concoctions. By day, the mood is a Lost in Translation-style hotel bar, with solitary guests nursing glasses of wine and nibbling on bar snacks, while by night the mood is riskier with lower lighting, live music – a singer followed by a DJ – and a cool cocktail crowd decked out in their designer finery that makes for a sexy scene. Highly recommended is the Devil's Tear by barman Anson Zhang. Made from yellow Chinese liquor, Chambord, Benedictine DOM, fresh lemon juice, syrup and a cinnamon stick as garnish, it'll have you swaying in the corridors as you pad your way back to your room. But enveloped within the beautiful bed that awaits, a hangover is certainly slept off in style. It's not just the building and what's packed so stylishly inside that makes China World Summit Wing, Beijing special. Service throughout is like a smooth, streamlined conveyor belt in a sushi joint, sweeping guests through the check-in process, orders at the bar and the restaurants, and anything else

149
150
151
152
153
154
155
156
157

CHINA

Top left
Executive Rooms offer spacious, comfortable and cosy elegance

Bottom left
The Ambassador Suite provides expansive space for work and relaxation

Above
The hotel offers plenty of opportunities for relaxation and rejuvenation

CHINA

Above
Sing Yin Cantonese Dining
serves Cantonese cuisine

Top right
Contemporary luxury is all
yours in the Fantastic Suite

Bottom right
The Extreme Wow Suite has
everything for a luxurious stay

W HONG KONG

HONG KONG, CHINA
COORDINATES: Ⓝ 22° 18' 17.6184" Ⓔ 114° 9' 38.4546"

Some places have an intangible wow factor and it's safe to say that W Hong Kong has put the W back into Wow. It prides itself on a refreshingly funky style and philosophy, and is no stranger to the Top Ten Trendiest Hotels in the World chart. A stone's throw away, at Kowloon Station, is perhaps the city's most lavish lifestyle shopping mall, Elements. Also, the highest indoor observation deck in Hong Kong, sky100, is connected to the hotel and is the place where you can soar high above the city on the 100th floor of the tallest building in town.
The Wow effect kicks in from the

moment you check in – there are touches of inspiration everywhere. On your way to your room, you walk through a corridor sculpted in white. In your room, the pre-set lighting adjusts to the time of day and the floor-to-ceiling windows are fabulous. The enormous bathroom has flattering back-lit mirrors, sliding walls that allow for extra privacy and there's even a built-in TV in the bath tub. The hotel is also known for its 9,000 square-metre BLISS® SPA on the 72nd floor that offers a dazzling array of treatments for men and women. Another noteworthy Discovery is the

"Wine-derlust" at the Living Room on Wednesday nights where guests can sample top-class wine and cheese from around the world in a thoroughly buzzing atmosphere. The hotel's pride and joy must not be missed however – WET®, the spectacular rooftop pool, affording staggering views over the harbour towards the island. The Wow effect continues with the hotel's newly launched poolside bar WET DECK, featuring W signature cocktails and scrumptious dishes. Wonderful with a capital W.

CHINA

Top left
Serenely tranquil surroundings of the Asian Tea Lounge at The Peninsula Spa by ESPA

Bottom left
The Roman-style swimming pool has harbour views of Hong Kong Island

Above
Rolls-Royce fleet at The Peninsula Hong Kong: style, quality and tradition

THE PENINSULA HONG KONG

HONG KONG, CHINA
COORDINATES: Ⓝ 22° 17' 43.0578" Ⓔ 114° 10' 18.3612"

The Peninsula Hong Kong opened in 1928 and has since been regarded as one of the most elegant and sophisticated hotels in the world. It deserves this accolade thanks to its sumptuous decor and exceptional views, through the picture-postcard windows in your suite and at The Peninsula Spa by ESPA, as well as at the swimming pool and sun terrace. The hotel commands spectacular views of Victoria Harbour and Hong

Felix restaurant, designed by Philippe Starck, serves modern European cuisine

Below
The Nadaman restaurant offers fine Japanese dining

Right
A Hong Kong panorama from a Harbour View Room

ISLAND SHANGRI-LA

HONG KONG, CHINA
COORDINATES: Ⓝ 22° 16' 36.354" Ⓔ 114E° 9' 51.7104"

From the moment you walk through the doors, to the moment you check out, your time and presence are considered precious at Island Shangri-La in Hong Kong. You'll be greeted by exceptionally friendly guest relations staff who quickly latch onto your personal tastes and greet you by name. As you mop your brow with a hot towel and sip Chinese tea served in your room, you quickly realise you're in excellent hands. You'll also notice a deliciously serene scent as you move around the public areas. Created especially for the hotel, it is suffused with delicate notes of ginger, bergamot, woods and vanilla.

From the impressive entrance, guests can take the lift to level 39 and change to the bubble lift to view the world's largest Chinese silk painting, the Great Motherland of China, hanging 51 metres into an atrium. There are more than 771 chandeliers throughout the hotel, including one in every guest room. All the rooms and suites are extremely spacious, fitted with beautiful Chinese antique furnishings, and boast incredible views of the city and Victoria Harbour or Victoria Peak. There are lovely touches everywhere, including L'Occitane toiletries in guest rooms and Bvlgari in suites. Every bathroom is fitted with a television, and the beds and pillows are superbly crisp and plump. Linen comes courtesy of Frette, so you'll sleep like a baby. The breakfast buffet at cafe TOO lays claim to being the best in the world, with its top quality service and freshest foods covering a wide range of world cuisines, including Japanese and traditional Chinese.

The Lobby lounge is a great place to sit, even for a solo traveller. Every day between 3pm and 7pm, a musical quartet entertains guests and you can have a bite to eat while listening to them play. Choose any national newspaper to catch up on world events or make the most of the free wi-fi available throughout the hotel and in the hotel's fleet of limousines, for those lucky enough to enjoy the chauffeur service, as well as in the rooftop Horizon Club. This state-of-the-art exclusive lounge is ideal for business travellers seeking peace as they contemplate the Hong Kong skyline and there's a 24-hour health club to keep up your fitness regime. As you order round-the-clock room service, you can't help thinking that the Island Shangri-La's mysterious perfumer managed to capture the very soul of this hotel, as its scent and memories linger on.

FUCHUN RESORT
HANGZHOU

ZHEJIANG, CHINA
COORDINATES: Ⓝ 30° 2' 55.8162" Ⓔ 119° 57' 36.612"

The Chinese character for "pavilion" signifies stopping for a rest, which is most appropriate for the Fuchun Resort. Located in the hills of Zhejiang province, the stress of city life seems remote. Its luxurious villas are situated on a hillside, overlooking mountains, streams and forest. The villas, which vary in size, create a labyrinth that makes its way down to a spectacular 18-hole golf course which, it has to be said, is a golfer's paradise. The golf course is only one in the region, and boasts a tea plantation and lake within its tranquil setting. Breakfast is a delicious time to start planning the day as you contemplate these panoramic views. Time stands still here, so it seems only right to enjoy a QI balancing massage in the Fuchun spa, a Himalayan yoga class or a dip in the indoor swimming pool and outdoor Jacuzzis.

149
150
151
152
153
154
155
156
157

CHINA

Above
The indoor swimming pool is complemented by outdoor Jacuzzis.

Top right
Peace and serenity are enhanced by lakes and mountains.

Bottom right
Villa accommodation offers privacy and complete tranquillity

Top left
Executive Corner Suites
provide space, comfort
and stunning views

Bottom left
CHI, The Spa offers
treatments to restore
balance and harmony

Above
Sydney Harbour and
Opera House are set against
the city skyline at night

SHANGRI-LA HOTEL, SYDNEY

SYDNEY, AUSTRALIA
COORDINATES: ⑤ 33° 51' 40.8708" Ⓔ 151° 12' 22.554"

It's hard to believe that The Rocks area of Sydney began life as an open-air jail. Totally transformed into a cosmopolitan area with a village atmosphere, it's now home to buzzing restaurants, boutique shops and the Shangri-La Hotel.
As a tourist in Sydney you simply can't beat the location of this luxury hotel.

and suites, and from the Altitude Restaurant and the 36th-floor Blu Bar, which incidentally serves arguably the best Martini in town.
It makes you wonder if anyone actually uses the large flat-screen televisions in their guest room when they can sit in the window and simply gaze at the iconic views.

Altitude Restaurant serves the finest contemporary Australian cuisine with spectacular views

Top left
The Lyall captures the essence of its chic address

Bottom left
The Champagne Bar has a fine selection of bubbly

Above
The Grand Suite for discerning guests and special occasions

LYALL HOTEL & SPA

MELBOURNE, AUSTRALIA
COORDINATES: (S) 37° 50' 16.5618" (E) 144° 59' 25.7136"

The Lyall in Melbourne stands on an elegant tree-lined street near the fashionable Toorak Road and Chapel Street. As the city's only privately owned and managed five-star hotel, it offers deluxe accommodation for a cosmopolitan clientele. Likened to an invisible embrace, the ambience is welcoming in a discreet club-like setting, where guests feel special, thanks to friendly and discerning 24-hour concierge service.

The tastefully appointed one and two-bedroom suites boast a living area, balcony, separate king bedroom and luxury bathroom. There are lovely touches, namely a gourmet minibar in the kitchen, stocked with delicious ice creams, and a mini art gallery on each floor where guests can lounge in front of the fire. Bistro Lyall has a world-class menu and the Champagne Bar offers an excellent selection of champagne by the bottle or flute. With the personalised treatments at the Lyall Spa and a Life Fitness gym, the chances are you'll never want to leave.

HAYMAN GREAT BARRIER REEF

QUEENSLAND, AUSTRALIA
COORDINATES: Ⓢ 20° 3′ 29.2602″ Ⓔ 148° 53′ 2.58″

Hayman is a private island which is part of the Whitsundays island chain christened by Captain Cook back in 1770 – and its astonishing beauty remains as unspoiled today. Landing here in your 50-foot luxury launch is like arriving with front-row tickets for one of the greatest shows on Earth – the Great Barrier Reef – surely the setting for a holiday in paradise. Guests come here to hide away in a haven of peace and soak up the surroundings. The choice of accommodation is as varied as it is luxurious with rooms, penthouses, beach villas and a

beach house which all enjoy private outdoor space and incredible views. The style is wonderfully fresh and contemporary with elegant sun loungers and pod lounges, where you can take your afternoon nap in the shade after a morning catamaran sailing or snorkeling.
There's something for everyone here, be it PADI diving courses, yacht cruises, helicopter rides and beach drops to secluded locations, golf practice or fabulously indulgent spa treatments. Food lovers are also in for a treat. Hayman's finest chefs offer

innovative and traditional menus in all the island's restaurants with contemporary Australian and international cuisine, after which it's tempting to follow the culinary classes laid on for guests. Simpler pleasures are just as memorable – take a walk along the beaches, through the botanic garden and across the rugged bushland. It's a breathtaking experience and confirms the award-winning Hayman's long-standing status as one of The Leading Hotels of the World.

AUSTRALIA

Above
Hayman is Australia's most-awarded five-star resort

Top right
Beach Villas have an abundance of natural light

Bottom right
The Hayman Pool's distinctive nautical design

NEW ZEALAND

Top left
Well-appointed Ridge Suites are spacious, comfortable and private

Bottom left
The Lodge is a modern marriage of rustic river stone and weathered wood

Above
The Loggia restaurant, under head chef Tim Pickering, serves fresh local produce

THE FARM AT CAPE KIDNAPPERS

HAWKE'S BAY, NEW ZEALAND
COORDINATES: Ⓢ 39° 38' 28.2012" Ⓔ 176° 59' 35.6784"

As exclusive luxury destinations go, there is no denying that The Farm at Cape Kidnappers is utterly unique in its concept, location and luxurious amenities. Nestled in Hawke's Bay, this lodge destination is ideal for exploring the natural landscape of ruggedly stunning beauty and the surrounding wine estates, for which this region is renowned. It's an extraordinary setting with a 6,000-acre cattle and sheep farm overlooking the Pacific Ocean. From the outside, the accommodation resembles a cluster of wonderfully preserved farm buildings. All 22 ultra-

comfortable and spacious Cottage Suites and the four-bedroom Owner's Cottage brim with character. The interior design is airy, spacious and welcoming. Chances are you'll never want to leave your beautifully appointed lounge and dining rooms, which have unparalleled views of the Pacific and the golf course. In fact, Cape Kidnappers has become a golf destination in its own right, earning a highly creditable 33rd place in Golf Magazine's ranking of all world-class golf courses.
Food and wine are serious business too with the Farm's gourmet à la carte

selection available at several of the lodge locations, and an excellent wine tasting room and wine cellar, stocked with top-class wines from New Zealand and beyond.
What adds to the special atmosphere here are the wonderful nooks and crannies that allow for utter peace and privacy. There are specific areas where guests can enjoy their own company while contemplating Hawke's Bay, Mount Ruapehu and the Mahia Peninsula. The Farm at Cape Kidnappers is truly the definition of a romantic and luxurious getaway.

EAGLES NEST

BAY OF ISLANDS , NEW ZEALAND
COORDINATES: Ⓢ 35° 15' 10.5798" Ⓔ 174° 6' 59.421"

Eagles Nest is luxury that quite deservedly holds a handful of industry awards for its flawless location and unsurpassable service. Set on its own 75-acre peninsula, overlooking the Bay of Islands, this extraordinary position allows guests to experience a truly customised service in the lap of luxury. There are just five private Villas all perfectly appointed with spacious living areas and heated horizon-edged pool, gourmet kitchen and a fabulous cinema system. You could be forgiven for never leaving your own private paradise.

So should you dream of a poolside barbecue or an in-villa nine-course dinner, prepared by fabulous resident chefs? Nothing is too much trouble for the exclusive concierge team. Also, lounge lizards will love the spa therapists on hand to provide in-villa treatments – how decadently lovely. We recommend that you step outside, however, for a taste of adventure in the Bay of Islands, which is world-renowned for its natural beauty and every type of water sport imaginable. Alternatively, why not

take a helicopter to the nearby golf course or to the spectacular winery? The concierge team will tailor your itinerary and ensure your stay is exactly as you want it.

There are so many memorable moments to enjoy here that the hardes decision you'll have to make is how to fit it all in. With its marine wildlife, clear blue water and secluded beaches, there is something for everyone in this remarkable piece of heaven.

Above
Cool Change is an exclusive sailing charter and unforgettable experience

Top right
Rahimoana Villa's day beds with infinity pool overlooking a private beach

Bottom right
Rahimoana epitomises the refined elegance of modern minimalism

THE AMERICAS

CONTENTS

Clayoquot Sound supports
wild salmon, rare species
and ancient giant cedar trees

166
167

CANADA

Above
Bedwell River is ideal for beginner and expert kayakers

Top right
Twenty guest tents offer unexpected comfort in the wilderness

Bottom right
The Cookhouse Outdoor Lounge is a place to relax and digest

CLAYOQUOT WILDERNESS RESORT

VANCOUVER ISLAND, CANADA
COORDINATES: Ⓝ 49° 9' 8.7618" Ⓦ 125° 54' 8.9748"

Your first glimpse of Clayoquot Wilderness Resort comes after a short flight from Vancouver, across a string of snow-covered peaks, descending into a valley of waterfalls, before touching down as a bear cub races across the field. As soon as you've stepped off the plane, you'll be greeted by managing directors, John and Adele, with a warm smile and a firm handshake. Right from the start, you know Clayoquot is not like other resorts – a family-run establishment, you feel as though you've been welcomed exclusively into

someone's luxury home.

With only 20 luxury tents in total, linked together by cedar boardwalks along the river estuary, Clayoquot promises intimacy. Here there are unexpected comforts in a remote wilderness and you'll find sanctuary in the great white canvas, prospector-style tents. You can lose yourself in the resort's lounge tents (the games and library tents). Their plush turn-of-the-century dark polished woods are an echo of old, familiar gentlemen's clubs. Warm and inviting

modern amenities are disguised within beautiful antique furnishings. Specialising in remarkable activities, you can find paradise while hiking across miles of surrounding wilderness or watch whales in the rolling waves of the Pacific Ocean. A favourite of guests at Clayoquot is horseback riding and, with a great stable of horses, the talented rider and beginner are in for a treat. What started with a handshake will conclude with hugs and kisses (and a tear) as you reluctantly leave the resort at the end of your stay.

The Lobby reflects the distinctive style of French designer Jacques Grange

Above
The Mark is a 1927 landmark building on the corner of 77th Street and Madison Avenue

Top right
Bedrooms offer comfort and modern convenience in the heart of Manhattan

Bottom right
Each Suite is a luxuriously serene retreat, decorated and furnished in 21st-century style

168
169

UNITED STATES

170
171
172
173
174
175
176
177
178
179

THE MARK

NEW YORK, UNITED STATES
COORDINATES: Ⓝ 40° 46' 30.8814" Ⓦ 73° 57' 48.5928"

When looking for the ultimate in Upper East Side chic, you should stroll directly to the corner of 77th and Madison Avenue where The Mark awaits you.

This location alone should give you a little insight into life at The Mark – overlooking Central Park, the treasures of The Frick are just down the block, while Christian Louboutin and Prada are right next door. Having opened in 1927 during the golden age of New York, The Mark has recently undergone a renovation by the celebrated Jacques Grange, who has restored this "grand dame" to her former Art Deco magnificence. You can imagine Greta Garbo sweeping into the glamorous black and white foyer for her appointment at Frédéric Fekkai, or Fred Astaire quietly sipping a Mark Manhattan in the seductive light of the bar designed by Guy de Rougemont.

In the bedrooms and suites, the latest Bang and Olufson video and audio technology has been discreetly masked behind the Parisian styling – think plush velvet sofas, soothing colours, black marble accents and deco lighting mixed with mirrored TV screens and window shades that close at the touch of a button.

But the real crowning glory of The Mark lies in the unique and unexpected details you will discover at every turn, from the handwritten notes left charmingly on your pillow, to the bespoke John Lobb shoe shine kiosk where guests can opt for The Mark Shine.

Old school charm combined with 21st-century cool – The Mark is one New York legend that is here to stay.

UNITED STATES

Top left
The Hudson Studio has stunning views over New York's riverfront

Bottom left
The Lobby expands on a century of modern design and architecture

Above
The Standard, New York is an emphatically non-standard hotel of the future

THE STANDARD, NEW YORK

NEW YORK, UNITED STATES
COORDINATES: N 40° 44' 27.1536" W 74° 0' 28.1556"

André Balazs' fourth Standard Hotel sits in New York's Meatpacking District, one of the city's most exciting neighbourhoods. The hotel's architecture blends vintage and modern style with great flair, and integrates beautifully within the city's landscape.

Needless to say, the views are breathtaking through the rooms' floor-to-ceiling windows, sweeping over the Empire State Building and "Lady Liberty" as well as arching over the High Line. The 18th-floor cocktail lounge has a spectacular 360-degree cityscape that offers a mesmerising backdrop to this 18-storey tower hotel. Catch the Sunset Service while you're there for an unforgettable evening. There's a fascinating mix of clientele, with locals and international guests reflecting the sophisticated atmosphere that makes this hotel a destination in its own right. The staff are renowned for their friendliness, professionalism and sense of humour. Nothing is too much trouble. If you need a late-night bite to eat, the kitchen is open round the clock. Michelin-star chef Dan Silverman –

Food and Wine magazine named him one of the ten best chefs – rustles up a fine menu for The Standard Grill restaurant, a nod to the traditional New York bar and grill.

Rooms are chic and comfortable for relaxing away from the buzz of the city. The Living Room bar and adjacent lobby have a DJ spinning the coolest tunes, and guests come here after dark for a taste of the city that never sleeps. The Standard, New York is a place you may never want to leave.

XV BEACON

BOSTON, UNITED STATES
COORDINATES: Ⓝ 42°21' 29.6964" Ⓦ 71° 3' 42.8358"

The elegant boutique hotel XV Beacon is a destination in its own right. Rich with history and character, the 1903 Beaux Arts landmark is situated atop Beacon Hill, one of Boston's most prestigious neighborhoods. Step through the opaque glass doors of the hotel and you're welcomed by attentive staff who remember your name from your first exchange.

Each of the distinctively appointed guest rooms and suites feels like home, and exudes an abundance of comfort – there's a gas fireplace which adds to the cozy charm. Perceptive and discreet service makes you feel like you are the only guest. Fresh fruit on every floor, newspapers of your choice delivered every morning, turndown service, 24-hour room service, complimentary wi-fi, Frette linens and a courtesy Lexus car service for within the city are all offered.

You won't drive too far though – the city's attractions are on the doorstep, and the hotel's cocktail lounge and restaurant cosset you in a relaxed ambience. The Mooo... Restaurant serves the most refined and mouthwatering steakhouse delicacies prepared by the award-winning chef and owner Jamie Mammano. Wine lovers should visit Mooo's private dining venue, The Wine Cellar, where the walls are lined with distinctive wines from around the world.

The mystique of XV Beacon is everywhere – in the service, the furnishings and the serene atmosphere. A unique feature is the hotel's art collection by some of the country's most renowned artists. This blends tradition with cutting-edge design. When in Boston, XV Beacon is the only place to be.

Above
The Beaux Arts landmark building stands on the crest of Beacon Hill

Top right
The Lobby reflects the chic modern design of this stylish boutique hotel

Bottom right
Corner Studio: sleek modern lines combine comfort and functionality

The south side of the Main
House, pictured in autumn,
looks out onto an upper
terrace and croquet lawn

Above
Fairlawn Guest Room
in the well-appointed
Carriage House

Top right
The Conservatory in the
Main House is used for
summertime breakfasts

Bottom right
Riverview Cottage's
comfortable sitting room
features a Hudson River mural

BLANTYRE

LENOX, UNITED STATES
COORDINATES: Ⓝ 42° 20′ 1″, Ⓦ 73° 15′ 8″

As you're tucking into afternoon-tea delicacies overlooking the manicured lawns, it's hard to believe you're in 21st-century America, halfway between Boston and New York. You could easily be in an English country house in a bygone era. Everything about Blantyre is a step back to a gentler, simpler time of old-world elegance and romance.

As you would expect from a member of Relais & Châteaux hotels, the food is a gourmet's dream come true, especially the exquisite five-course

tasting menu and special wine dinners. In spring, enjoy a luxurious picnic lunch – think homemade breads, iced tea and lobster – in the hotel grounds, complete with tablecloth and cushions. In winter, enjoy the unique snow barbecues serving up robust comfort food and the most delicious fig and orange bread pudding. The wine cellar can compete with those found in the wine regions of Europe and the sommelier has a passion for wine that is truly contagious.

If you happen to have some time not consumed by eating and drinking, then don't miss indulging in a treatment at the quaintly named Potting Shed Spa; try your hand at croquet or ice skating on the hotel's own skating rink; or simply wander around the 115 acres of beautiful gardens and woodland. The attention to detail throughout the hotel and extraordinary personalised service you'll receive will ensure you feel completely at home and totally relaxed. In fact, you'll probably be planning dates when you can return

The Brazilian Court is the ultimate Florida destination for the rich and famous

Above
Studios and suites are appointed in luxurious colonial style

Top right
Living areas offer a wealth of comfort and private amenities

Bottom right
Café Boulud is a warm and welcoming French-American venue

168
169
170
171
172
173
174
175

UNITED STATES

176
177
178
179

THE BRAZILIAN COURT HOTEL & BEACH CLUB

PALM BEACH, UNITED STATES
COORDINATES: Ⓝ 26° 42' 12.114" Ⓦ 80° 2' 19.4922"

It's easy to see why The Brazilian Court Hotel & Beach Club has been a glamorous hideaway for the rich and famous since the 1920's. Cloaked in European old-world charm, the hotel retains a sense of old-fashioned romance coupled with modernity following its loving and extensive renovation.

The hotel boasts a loyal and impossibly glamorous clientele who appreciate The Brazilian Court's qualities. For example, there's round-the-clock butler service and luxurious professional staff who make this haven a home away from home. The hotel is the destination of choice for Palm Beachers to house their guests – clearly a good sign. Notably Rose Kennedy, matriarch of the America's premier political family, used to check her guests in here.

The plush accommodation includes studios as well as one, two and three-bedroom suites. The furniture and tapestries are custom-made and every guest space features sleek flat-screen plasma LCD TVs, ultra hydro-thermo massage menus. Epicureans are in for a treat with every detail carefully considered. There's the award-winning Café Boulud and the Frederic Fekkai Salon & Spa, as well as an Author Breakfast Series and an art gallery featuring the work of Mark Bowles. You can imagine the likes of Fred Astaire, Ingrid Bergman and Audrey Hepburn retiring to their private terrace and secret garden to watch the sun set over Palm Beach – and if it was good enough for them...

168
169
170
171
172
173
174
175
176
177
178
179

UNITED STATES

Top left
The Penthouse double living room overlooks the Atlantic Ocean

Bottom left
Bi-level Suites achieve a separation of living space and bedroom

Above
The Grill's award-winning wine cellar complements European cuisine

THE SETAI SOUTH BEACH, MIAMI

MIAMI, UNITED STATES
COORDINATES: Ⓝ 25° 47' 46.4598", Ⓦ 80° 7' 42.8514"

South Beach Miami immediately conjures up images of beautiful beaches, equally beautiful people and endless sunshine. It's a destination synonymous with pleasure and partying. But we're not all 24-7 party people and, when you need some downtime, you can't beat the Zen-like tranquillity of The Setai. The hotel is elegant, and you're treated to second-to-none Asian hospitality throughout the property. Spend your days snoozing on the super-comfortable daybeds by one of the pools or on the beach. Or recharge your body and mind in the spa. Soak up the ambiance of peace and serenity. Before you head out to explore the sizzling South Beach

THE BETSY HOTEL

MIAMI, UNITED STATES
COORDINATES: Ⓝ 25° 47' 11.526" Ⓦ 80° 7' 46.5558"

The Betsy is a distinguished landmark in a town where flamboyance is generally the order of the day. The hotel stands proud on Ocean Drive along Miami's South Beach and, behind its colonial facade, lies a haven of peace with just 61 tasteful and understated rooms and suites. For a creative touch and sensory details, you're in for a treat here. Fresh orchids grace every room, while the inspirational design marries contemporary style and state-of-the-art technology with elegant touches of yesteryear.

There are stunning ocean views from the rooms and why not plan a trip to the beach with a specially prepared picnic hamper courtesy of the butler service? A courtyard pool is located off the airy lobby in an atmosphere that is quintessential "salon". From floor to ceiling, The Betsy offers an intimate retreat from the coastline, with tasteful touches of traditional colonial splendour.

The Deck at The Betsy is an expansive rooftop with sweeping views of the Atlantic coast adorned with palm trees. A Zen-inspired calm comes through with natural materials, like wood decking, stone and bamboo, all shielded by retractable sails. The Wellness Spa offers treatments, therapies and yoga in a location that's therapeutic in itself.

Wile away the hours on the rooftop with speciality cocktails, try a light meal at the lobby bar or go for Laurent Tourondel's refined take on the iconic American steakhouse. You'll be dreaming of your stay at The Betsy, far from the madding crowd, for a long time to come – and planning your next visit.

168
169
170
171
172
173
174
175
176
177
UNITED STATES
178
179

Above
Betsy Grand Suites feature comfortable contemporary colonial design

Top right
The hotel is an historic landmark on Miami Beach's famed Ocean Drive

Bottom right
BLT Steak is a modern American steakhouse with a French flavour

Shutters on the Beach is just grains of sand away from the ocean

Above
Coast café and patio bar
is a relaxed place to eat or
enjoy a cocktail

Top right
Ocean View Guest Room:
wake up to the sound of
the surf

Bottom right
The Pacific Terrace is
a shady retreat from the
pool and the sun

168
169
170
171
172
173
174
175
176
177
178
179

UNITED STATES

SHUTTERS ON THE BEACH

SANTA MONICA, UNITED STATES
COORDINATES: Ⓝ 34° 0' 24.357" Ⓦ 118° 29' 30.0942"

Relaxed yet refined, Shutters on the Beach is the epitome of Californian laid-back luxury. Undeniably beautiful, Shutters is both casual and sophisticated, evoking a sense of carefree chic. The location is unbeatable, sitting right on the edge of Santa Monica beach and looking straight towards a never-ending stretch of sea and sky. It's a glorious water pervades the whole building, giving the hotel a relaxed, airy feel. The hotel almost feels like a private seaside retreat, each guest room offering a small library of books, a cosy reading chair and rich hardwood flooring. Head up to the Pacific Terrace for views along the coast or simply pull up a deck chair and watch the world go by. A five-star haven of buzz of live jazz floating around the Living Room, creating an atmosphere of casual elegance. Follow your nose and excite your taste buds at either of the impeccable restaurants serving American market-fresh fare and fabulous wines, including several favourites from up-state Napa Valley. What's more, there's a lavish spa on site to top it all off. This is American

Top left
Altamira Reflecting Pool: a
night vista to excite the senses

Bottom left
Remède Spa creates an
exceptional experience

Above
Jack Nicklaus has designed
two signature golf courses her

THE ST. REGIS
PUNTA MITA RESORT

PUNTA MITA, MEXICO
COORDINATES: Ⓝ 20° 46' 9.735" Ⓦ 105° 32' 18.5532"

The St. Regis Punta Mita Resort is
Latin America's first St. Regis hotel
and it does the brand proud. It enjoys a
stunning location on one of the world's
most alluring beaches and its exquisite
grounds include two Jack Nicklaus
golf courses, three infinity pools and a
sumptuous word-class Remède Spa.
The hotel is the latest in the St. Regis
group to continue the tradition of
its signature butler service – a truly
personal round-the-clock service,
and trademark of the company and
its hotels worldwide. Rightfully
described as heaven on Earth, the

experience starts as soon as you check
in. Your St. Regis butler takes care of
carrying the luggage to your room as
well as unpacking and settling you in
to your accommodation.
The resort consists of a series of
buildings, spread over a large acreage
of land, and 89 rooms, 31 luxurious
suites and a three-bedroom
presidential suite.
Start your day with breakfast around
the pool at Las Marietas with Mexican
and American specialities, including the
highly recommended Nayarit Breakfast
– pastries, fruit and eggs rancheros.

It's easy to spend your days lounging
around the three pools – one is
specifically for families – where staff
are on hand to bring you a margarita
cocktail and fresh tacos.
Food lovers are in for a treat with Las
Marietas serving authentic Mexican
cuisine, The Sea Breeze Beach Club
dishing up contemporary Californian
cuisine and the resort's Five Diamond
award-winning Signature Restaurant
Carolina offering an exotic selection
of world-class seafood.

LAS ALCOBAS MEXICO DF

MEXICO CITY, MEXICO
COORDINATES: Ⓝ 19° 25' 54.0768" Ⓦ 99° 11' 52.7562"

Las Alcobas in Mexico City's fashionable district of Polanco tops the bill for luxury. This boutique hotel outshines any would-be rivals with its blend of style, discretion and round-the-clock butler service. What strikes you first? Is it the impeccable understated luxury and attention to detail? Or maybe it's the refreshingly personal and accommodating approach by the hotel staff? Certainly the philosophy is terrifically successful – to create a luxury urban hotel that feels like a private home. A former apartment complex, Las Alcobas has evolved into a collection of meticulously crafted, intimate alcoves, rooms or alcobas. The design is elegant simplicity featuring the finest linens, full-length mirrors, high-powered hairdryers, well-equipped desks for busy professionals, a mini-bar stocked with local snacks and candies, and wake-up calls with tea or coffee. All bathrooms are mini spas complete with locally sourced handmade toiletries.

For a full-on experience, the hotel's Aurora Spa offers a great range of indulgent signature treatments. Tequila experts are treated to arguably the best selection of tequila for miles around. And the treat continues over dinner. Be sure to book one of the hottest tables in town at the Dulce Patria, overseen by Mexico's highly acclaimed chef Martha Ortiz, or (from early-2012) at Anatole, under the expertise of chef Justin Ermini.

Above
The hotel lobby reflects the style of designers Yabu Pushelberg

Top right
Bedrooms and bathrooms are infused with warmth and texture

Bottom right
Guest-room living areas combine modern convenience with comfort

Top left
Two-storey cottages, within the estate's tropical garden, have private pools

Bottom left
The Rosa Ocean View Master Suite features a domed brick Catalan ceiling

Above
Esencia Beach: idyllic white sands lapped by the deep-blue Caribbean

ESENCIA ESTATE

RIVIERA MAYA, MEXICO
COORDINATES: Ⓝ 20° 28' 42.46" Ⓦ 87° 15' 11.76"

Esencia is located on one of the most beautiful beaches in the Riviera Maya in Mexico. Situated in a 50-acre private estate, this extraordinary place is so much more than a hotel, with its awe-inspiring beachfront, two swimming pools, day spa and gourmet restaurant. It has a certain regal cachet that comes from being the erstwhile retreat for an Italian duchess and all that this entails – impeccable style, service and setting. Guests staying here are in for holiday of a lifetime. Treated as if you're in the Italian duchess' private home,

you receive an entirely personalised service. Staff instantly know you by name and remember the important details that make you feel special, like how you drink your coffee or what room temperature you prefer. There are 29 ocean and garden view rooms, suites and cottages, of which 19 have private pools. The finishings are crafted from native woods, the spaces are bright and airy, with high ceilings, and mahogany louvered doors open onto tropical gardens and sea views. Dining is an equally memorable

experience with a choice of gourmet delicacies prepared with fresh local ingredients and presented with the utmost elegance. If you fancy being royally pampered, Aroma is the first organic spa on the Riviera Maya to use pure indigenous fruits, plants and herbs, many of which are sourced from the hotel's garden. The organic treatments deploy ancient Mayan techniques in the massages, herbal facials and saunas. Like every aspect of Esencia, they are fit for a king or queen

CUIXMALA

JALISCO, MEXICO
COORDINATES: Ⓝ 19° 22' 29.8086" Ⓦ 105° 0' 32.1978"

Originally the private estate of financier Sir James Goldsmith, this expanse of idyllic beaches and mysterious lagoons is the ideal destination for those craving tranquillity. The lush vegetation that surrounds Cuixmala is a haven for exotic animals and thousands of birds. Take a boat tour around the lagoon and spot zebras, white tail deer and coati mundis. With three private beaches, plus surfing, diving and fishing, you'll never want to get out of the blue water. Luckily, the Cuixmala staff barbeque fresh seafood right on the beach, so you'll never have to. The accommodation is plush, ranging from the palatial Casa La Loma to the cosy Casitas, perfect for families or groups of friends. For tranquillity and stunning ocean views, the luxurious Casa La Loma and three glorious Villas will tick all the boxes. From splash-pool-size Jacuzzis and tropical gardens with a private beach, to cooks, butlers and acres of space for families, you'll want for nothing.

The location is home to the ecologically important Chamela-Cuixmala Biosphere Reserve as well as being ideal for surfing, hiking trails, horse riding lessons, scuba diving, boat trips and something truly special, Cuixmala's Turtle Protection Programme. This is a rare and unforgettable opportunity to assist in the protection of the giant sea turtles that lay their eggs in the sands of Playa Cuixmala. Staff collect the eggs, protecting them from poachers and other predators, and release the hatched baby turtles into the sea. Memories to stay with you forever.

Above
The Casitas are a cluster of charming small houses in a lush tropical garden

Top right
Casa La Loma: cool chic and unashamed luxury by the ocean

Bottom right
A bedroom at the Villa Torre: an infinity pool overlooks a coconut plantation

The Resort and Estate are on the windward side of Canouan Island in beautiful, protected bays

Above
The Caribbean Sea is the backdrop for quiet seclusion

Top right
Villas with a sea view also have private swimming pools

Bottom right
The Spa has its roots in the ancient search for eternal youth

CANOUAN RESORT & THE GRENADINES ESTATE VILLAS

GRENADINES, CARIBBEAN
COORDINATES: Ⓝ 12° 43' 3.8064" Ⓦ 61° 19' 24.8982"

Canouan Resort & the Grenadines Estate Villas lie at the heart of The Grenadines in the south-eastern Caribbean, 20 minutes from Barbados and St Lucia. Everything about this resort spells relaxation as it covers two-thirds of Canouan, essentially making it a private island with lagoons and secluded surroundings. A collection of stunning two to seven-bedroom Villas, with private pools, are dotted among hidden coves and beautiful white beaches. Coral reefs provide excellent diving and there are plenty of water sports, as well as tennis and golf with a stunning 18-hole championship golf course regarded as one of the best in the world. The view from the 13th hole is particularly spectacular. Elsewhere, the four signature restaurants offer a great choice of fine cuisine, and your wine will be chilled and served to perfection.

The team of attentive staff pride themselves on the ultimate personalised service for each and every guest. Your glass will never be empty by the pool and they'll remember your name. The 24-hour concierge service ensures that every detail goes to plan, so you can just get on with enjoying your holiday to the full. When booking a Suite or Villa you can include a Jet transfer to the resort, in true James Bond style, on weekends for all seven-night stays. And be sure to visit Tobago Cays, as well as book a treatment at the Canouan Resort Spa for full-on indulgence.

CARIBBEAN

Top left
Pool Pavilions feature a
12-metre infinity pool
bordered by teak decking

Bottom left
Amanyara enjoys a secluded
location with white sand beach
and rocky coves

Above
Beach Villas have direct
access to a private beach
and turquoise waters

AMANYARA

TURKS & CAICOS ISLANDS, CARRIBEAN
COORDINATES: Ⓝ 21° 49' 44.6442", Ⓦ 72° 20' 21.8292"

The Amanyara lives up to its name
which is derived from the Sanskrit
for "peaceful place". This exquisite
spot, located in the Turks and Caicos,
is surrounded by breathtaking views.
Landing here is like stepping into
heaven – pavilions and villas that
overlook the oceanfront or tranquil
ponds, or are nestled within lush island

unrivalled ocean views, and fine local
and Asian cuisine. The new Nature
Discovery Centre is great for adults
and families, and is the perfect place
to go diving, snorkelling or explore the
natural beauty of the island. Staying
at The Amanyara is all about turning
off the stress and tuning into nature
on your own time. Not a tough call in

GAIA HOTEL & RESERVE

MANUEL ANTONIO, COSTA RICA
COORDINATES: Ⓝ 9° 25' 03.69" Ⓦ 84° 09' 24.65"

Gaia Hotel is nestled high above Costa Rica's dramatic Pacific coastline. This five-star boutique hotel offers so much more than luxury and beautiful scenery in lush surroundings. It might interest you to know that it's also an adults-only hotel and resort designed for guests who are looking to totally escape to a tropical paradise.

The design is sleek, modern and environmentally friendly with more than a nod to Bauhaus. All the rooms are surrounded by jungle or ocean – the hardest thing is choosing which view to plump for. Once settled, you really can leave all your worries behind because you'll be assigned a personal concierge to cater for your every need around the clock. They will help you choose the best places to visit and arrange your excursions, take care of your room service and ensure that every day is a dream come true.

To really make the most of your "me time", spend your afternoons by the three-tiered infinity pool where you can enjoy the unique in-water table dining and contemplate the horizon.

Spa lovers will spend many an hour in The Terra Spa where there are six treatment rooms and dozens of exotic therapies to wile away a lazy morning before lunch. La Luna restaurant serves exceptional cuisine, featuring international and local dishes; special dietary requirements can be accommodated. Whatever you do, don't miss Gaia's Nature Reserve guided tour to catch a glimpse of the wonderful three-toed sloths and red-eyed tree frogs.

Above
The pool area, pictured at night, is on two levels, connected by a cascading waterfall

Top right
A private terrace for alfresco dining and romantic evenings watching the sun set.

Bottom right
The luxurious Villa living and dining area offers spacious comfort away from home

Below
Shamash Healing Space
SPA is a tranquil place
to rejuvenate

Right
The Pool, lined by palm
trees, overlooks a white
sandy beach

TXAI RESORT

BAHIA, BRAZIL
COORDINATES: Ⓢ 14° 23' 0.1314" Ⓦ 39° 0' 40.3446"

Situated on Itacarezinho Beach among the swaying coconut palms, with the mountains as a backdrop, lies the luxurious Txai Resort Itacaré. It's a wondrous place, enveloped by the most astounding landscape and rich culture, so throw away any pre-conceived ideas about luxury and nature. This resort has everything to do with beauty, relaxation and exceptional service, and nothing to do with bling and excess.

The architecture, inspired by the old cocoa plantation houses, is a successful blend of charm and rustic Bahia appeal that seamlessly integrates nature with the buildings. The collection of bungalows, suspended on stilts over wooden terraces, offers a romantic space and encapsulates an original type of bucolic luxury, with thatched roofing, spacious verandahs, king-size beds and a stunning outdoor shower area that is totally private.

Your days here are heavenly as you can lounge by one of the five pools or on the beach with butler service to cater for your every need (there is also round-the-clock room service). There is precious little chance that you'll feel tense but, should you wish to sample the pleasures of utter indulgence, the resort has a spa that's no ordinary treatment centre. Shamash Healing Space takes pampering to a whole new level of enjoyment. Apart from the holistic approach to soothing the body and soul, check out the views. This hilltop location overlooks the ocean and commands astounding panoramic vistas. We think there's no other way to spend an afternoon here, after a massage, than to take it all in on a lounger chair and sip on some coconut water before taking a dip in the plunge pool.

When you can bring yourself to leave this haven of peace – it won't be easy – you should try out the food on offer. There's a delicious fusion of Bahia, Brazilian and European cuisine that prides itself on an organic and healthy approach to eating. There are three restaurants to choose from – poolside, on the beach or on the hill surveying the land. As you contemplate the setting, it's worth planning an expedition, organised by your butler, to the Atlantic Forest. Don't leave without discovering the secret waterfalls, wild beaches, mangroves and local craftwork that make the experience of staying at Txai Resort Itacaré so memorable – how luxury and nature can live together in perfect harmony.

POUSADA ESTRELA D'ÁGUA

BAHIA, BRAZIL
COORDINATES: Ⓢ 16° 34' 51.6102" Ⓦ 39° 5' 21.6024"

Whatever you desire most in a luxuriously relaxing holiday, the Pousada Estrela D'Água will deliver. Located in the village of Trancoso, this is the place to be for some colourful Brazilian culture. Bordered by mangroves, alive with exotic birds and flowers, and flanked by the white sands of Nativos Beach, the charming little hotel blends seamlessly into its natural surroundings. Rooms feature wooden furnishings and crisp white linen. Master Suites have private Jacuzzis or swimming pools while Suites have private terraces with hammocks.

Chef Neca Menna Barreto has created the menu in the resort's two restaurants, offering traditional Bahian and international cuisine. In the Aldeia de São João restaurant, the breakfasts are as sensational as the views. Order fresh fruit salad, natural yoghurt, tapioca and the typical Bahian sweet, cocada, a delicious sugary, coconut creation.

Not to be missed are the hotel's organised diving expeditions and kayak tours through the mangroves. For a truly unforgettable experience, take a boat trip to watch the whales playing in the Atlantic before they start their migratory journey. Golfers enjoy special green-fee rates at the Terravista Golf Club adjacent to the hotel. Arguably Latin America's best golf course, it extends to the Trancoso cliffs, where the ocean views are unmissable.

After such an eventful day, it's time to enjoy a complimentary footbath, followed by an invigorating treatment at the hotel's spa. Finally, sip a fruit caipirinha – the hotel's signature cocktail – and relax as the glowing sun sets on the never-ending horizon.

Above
Master Suites are air-conditioned bungalows with private pool or Jacuzzi

Top right
Master Duplex Suites are air-conditioned bungalows with an ocean view

Bottom right
The swimming pool and sun deck offer fun and relaxation

Below
Stairway to Heaven - and to
a first-wave eco-chic resort

Right
Luxurious private villas are
situated at the ocean's edge

188
189
190
191

BRAZIL

KENOA – EXCLUSIVE BEACH SPA & RESORT

ALAGOAS, BRAZIL
COORDINATES: ⓈＳ 9° 48' 8.2686", Ⓦ 35° 51' 37.7676"

On the beautiful north-east coast of Barra de São Miguel, Kenoa – Exclusive Beach Spa & Resort overlooks a glorious green sea peppered with coral reefs, dense mangroves and five kilometres of nature reserve. It's obvious why Kenoa's innovative interior designer drew inspiration from its stunning natural surroundings. The contrasting materials used throughout the resort – think polished wood alongside rough brick – blur boundaries with the great outdoors. The trunks of reforested eucalyptus trees, which seemingly grow through the floors and roofs as if the hotel were part of the surrounding mangroves, are unexpected and extraordinary. But, although Kenoa is an original expression of its surroundings, the raw materials used at the resort – sourced from places as far flung as Bali, China, the Amazon and Central Africa – symbolise a wider environment.

Kenoa's owner Pedro Marques is confident that the resort can be sustainable, without compromising on service or luxury. And this is so, if the locally produced food served in the Kaamo Restaurant is anything to go by. With energy-saving LED lights, recycled glass bottles and non-ironed staff uniforms, Kenoa really is an eco-chic retreat.

The rooms at Kenoa Resort maintain this friendly relationship with nature. The Apoena Suites and the Araxá Suite stand high above the neighbouring nature reserve, with stunning views of the ocean. Closer to the ground, located right on the beach, are the Marajó and Jaobi Villas, and the exclusive Kenoa Villa is an eccentric residence completely in harmony with its surroundings. The villas boast fabulous, heated private plunge pools which, thanks to their remarkable Balinese stone finishing, create the illusion of stretching into

the sea and to the horizon beyond. They also offer spacious living areas appointed with the latest technology and luxuries to make you feel utterly special – king-size beds with Egyptian cotton sheets, double vanity bathroom basins, writing desk, CD and DVD player, wi-fi internet.

A cool sea breeze compliments Kenoa's tropical climate perfectly and the water is always a lovely temperature. The Kenoa Spa offers exclusive treatments where all five senses are pampered, and the Kaamo Restaurant, Winebar & Lounge is an extra sensory treat. Headed by world-renowned chef César Santos, the restaurant serves a delicious range of local cuisine – try the specialties cooked in a traditional Portuguese Cataplana dish.

We're sure that any preconceptions you may have about eco-friendly living will completely change when you visit the extraordinary Kenoa – Exclusive Spa & Resort.

INSOLITO BOUTIQUE

RIO DE JANEIRO, BRAZIL
COORDINATES: Ⓢ 22° 46′ 9.8796″ Ⓦ 41° 52′ 58.5834″

Two hours north of Cidade Maravilhosa, Insolito Boutique Hotel is the brainchild of French-born Emmanuelle Meeus de Clermont-Tonnerre. This luxury hotel shines with an artful blend of tropical flora, Portuguese stone, terracotta tiling and two-storey glass panelling.

Inside, the hotel's 20 rooms and suites tell a story of Brazil's colourful past that is exquisitely rendered with bespoke objets du désir – a George Nelson chair here, a wooden sofa sculpture by Elma Chavez there, parquet floors and a crimson lampshade, reflected in sweeping floor-to-ceiling windows that open out onto a veranda with a whirlpool and an ocean view to die for.

Come the evening, after a swim in the seawater pool or treatment at the wellness centre, guests can sample a Cachaça at the American bar. By night Brazilian-French fusion cuisine is paired with an international wine list and a very attentive smile at the hotel's rooftop restaurant.

Above
The hotel is located on the edge of one of the most beautiful beaches in Búzios

Top right
Thematic rooms, decorated with designer objects, immerse guests in Brazilian culture

Bottom right
The swimming pool hugs the coastline and is a place of relaxation and pleasure

Overlooking Lake Toro and the
Paine Massif, Patagonia Camp
is a unique luxury experience

Above
Yurts are comfortable and
independent domed tents

Top right
Well-appointed, yurts have all
facilities and luxury bathrooms

Bottom right
The Bar is a place to relax,
unwind and enjoy the views

PATAGONIA CAMP

TORRES DEL PAINE NATIONAL PARK, CHILE
COORDINATES: Ⓢ 51° 16' 59.8008" Ⓦ 72° 50' 21.7104"

In the wilds of mythical Patagonia, hidden away from the trappings of modern life, lies a treasure for the adventurous traveller looking for a soupcon of luxury thrown into the "great outdoors" experience. Patagonia Camp in Chile will simply blow you away. It's a luxury tented camp that's so much more than you would expect, as it was designed and built to have minimum impact on the environment. The entire complex is at one with the landscape. Built on wooden stilts and platforms, it features yurts and communal areas connected by walkways. Nature lovers will be heartened to know that centuries-old flora, fauna and trees, as well as wildlife communities, are protected by responsible waste treatment programmes.

The accommodation consists of 18 luxury yurts with private bathrooms and terraces, and comfortable king-size or twin beds, all overlooking the Paine Massif and turquoise waters of Lake Toro. One building serves as a restaurant, bar and lounge, connected by elevated walkways which create a magically intimate effect.

Dining in the Quincho is truly memorable as you get a hands-on feel for your food. The chef combines deliciously fresh regional produce like lamb, tasty southern hake, juicy fruit and vegetables. We recommend the famous Patagonia barbecue of slow-roasted Magallanic lamb which is so healthy and out of this world. A glass of fine Chilean wine to wash it down and who said that a trekking expedition across the Torres del Paine was tricky?

Surrounded by mountains and lakes, the hotel has heated indoor and outdoor pools

Above
An 18-hole golf course
is framed by Patagonian
mountains

Top right
Deluxe Moreno bathrooms
feature Jacuzzis and
breathtaking views

Bottom right
The Main Lobby offers
a warm welcome to
Argentine Patagonia

LLAO LLAO HOTEL & RESORT GOLF SPA

RÍO NEGRO, ARGENTINA
COORDINATES: Ⓢ 41° 3' 28.242" Ⓦ 71° 31' 52.7016"

The picture-postcard location of Llao Llao Hotel & Resort Golf Spa is second-to-none, nestled among the cypress woods, snow-covered mountains and crystal-clear lakes of the unspoilt Nahuel Huapi National Park in Argentine Patagonia. The resort is cleverly designed to blend into these impressive surroundings with the scenery visible throughout the property.

There are so many breathtaking and unique experiences to make your stay here truly unforgettable.

From the simplest things, such as the remarkable view from your breakfast table and the traditional Llao Llao afternoon tea served in the Winter Garden, to a dip in the outdoor infinity pool overlooking the snow-capped mountains, as the steam rises from the water, and a round of golf surrounded by the imposing Patagonian mountains and crystalline lakes. You can't fail to be captivated.

This is not a resort where you will experience boredom. Spend your days at one with the surrounding nature, be

it on a mountain-bike tour, kayaking or fly-fishing in one of the nearby lakes, trekking or skiing the Llao Llao mountain range. Or for a fun insight into the local culture, take tango lessons. At the end of the day, revitalise your tired limbs with a hot-stone massage in the spa before retreating to a comfortable chair by the fireplace in the lounge, with a glass of Argentinean wine, to ponder your next memorable day of adventure and exploration.

Eolo is a unique place that
embodies the spirit and
indigenous roots of Patagonia

Above
Terrace view of La Anita valley on the eastern side of Mount Frías

Top right
Horse riding is available at different levels of expertise and duration

Bottom right
Spacious Corner Suites enjoy views of the 3,000-hectare property

EOLO – PATAGONIA'S SPIRIT

SANTA CRUZ, ARGENTINA
COORDINATES: Ⓢ 50°20' 26.4624" Ⓦ 72° 27' 47.991"

It's hard to believe you're just an hour from Glaciers Natural Park and close to the national airport as you contemplate the peaceful beauty of Eolo. This stunning setting graces the Patagonian steppe with a sense of style and exclusivity surrounded by an enormous expanse of breathtaking natural landscape.

With its 17 suites, Eolo offers luxurious accommodation with a remarkable concierge service which allows guests to discover and dip into the Patagonian way of life.
Designed in a simple style, inspired by the utilitarian architecture of Patagonian estancias, all rooms and common areas are furnished with a mixture of modern and antique pieces, and boast exceptional views overlooking lakes, mountains and glaciers as well as the steppe.
The staff are exceptional with an unpretentious and flexible approach to service. From the moment you arrive, you'll be greeted by name and the team will see to it that you feel utterly at home day and night.
Every activity and detail here is simply delivered to emphasise the purity of the location, and its traditions and riches. Outdoor activities can be arranged, and there's something for everyone with trekking, bird watching, mountain bike and horse riding, courtesy of expert host guides. We especially recommend a boat trip to the spectacular glaciers and the four-wheel drive expeditions cross country. Eolo's setting lends itself so well to serious relaxation, with a sauna, indoor heated pool and even a well stocked library for enlightened contemplation.

HEAD OF EDITORIAL

EDITOR

WRITERS

Nathalie Grainger graduated in theatre arts from Leeds University and is bi-lingual in English and French. She has 20 years' experience in translation, interpreting and writing for European magazines, newspapers and institutions in Brussels. She has also written a number of websites for luxury perfume brands in both English and French. Her philanthropic values and passion for writing culminated in the founding of a theatre company in Brussels for disadvantaged children, helping them to explore the power of the written word as a means of expression and interaction. Previously she was the author of Quintessentially Perfume and Quintessentially Living, Volume II. She has a passion for travel, languages and perfume.

Peter Archer is an award-winning freelance writer and editor who was formerly a senior correspondent with the Press Association national news agency. His specialisms are varied, ranging from hotels, travel and lifestyle to finance, sustainability and the environment. He is a regular editor of Raconteur Supplements in *The Times*, as well as Prince William's biographer and a former adviser to the American TV network NBC. Assignments have taken him around the world several times and he has also been a war correspondent.

Frédérique Andreani is the editor of London lifestyle online magazine *Chic-Londres* and the UK correspondent for French magazine *Le Point*. She has lived in London since 1999 during which time she has written a London guide published in France. She was born in Paris, where she studied history and politics, and lives in Kensal Green with her two daughters Blanche and Galliane.

Nick Clarke was asked at the age of seven what he wanted to do when he was older. His answer: "Travel the world." He pretty much got his wish, diving head-first into the world of travel writing for a number of magazines and newspapers. With a passion for first-class seats, mile-high champagne, Michelin-starred restaurants and fine thread-count sheets, he loves nothing more than packing his suitcase and heading to the airport.

Polly Crossman first fell in love with travelling, aged 17, on a month-long trip to Bolivia. Since then her travels have taken her across Europe and to India, China and South-East Asia. After graduating from Durham University with a degree in English literature, she spent a year contributing to a number of travel publications and continues to work as a freelance writer, while specialising in public relations for the luxury travel industry.

Harry Hughes is a romantic soul whose love of travel encapsulates his joie de vivre. Currently the editor at Quintessentially, he has written on luxury travel for several years, voyaging to numerous far-flung places in the process. His work has appeared in several esteemed publications, from *The Times* to *Quintessentially Magazine*, and continues to gather popularity. A lover of poetry, hats and coffee, you'll usually find him with his guitar, playing the music he loves.

Scott Manson is an award-winning journalist who has edited British Airways *High Life* and *NetJets*, the magazine for owners of private jets. He has contributed travel and lifestyle features to publications including *Sunday Times Style*, *Sunday Times Travel*, *Daily Mail*, *Evening Standard*, *FHM*, *Men's Health*, *Music Week*, and *Adventure Travel*. He is also a former columnist for *London Lite* newspaper.

Josh Sims is a London-based freelance writer, who has contributed to publications including *The Financial Times*, *The Times*, *The Independent*, *Esquire*, and *Wallpaper*. He is editor of the social trends journal *Viewpoint* and an author. His latest book is *Icons of Men's Style*. As well as feature articles on travel and hotels, he has written entertainingly on curry, donkeys, chat-up lines and trousers.

ACCESSING
REMOTE
LOCATIONS

MOUNTAIN RETREATS

MAGICAL
MOMENTS

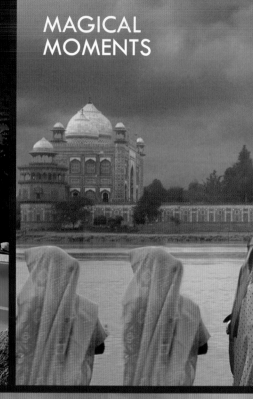

AWE-INSPIRING

PRIVATE AND
PERSONALISED

 QT QUINTESSENTIALLY TRAVEL

UNRIVALLED
EXPERIENCES

UNIQUE ACCOMMODATION

PARADISE ISLANDS

PROPERTY INDEX

- ▬ EUROPE
- ▬ AFRICA & INDIAN OCEAN
- ▬ MIDDLE EAST, ASIA & PACIFIC
- ▬ THE AMERICAS

204

INDEX

205
206
207
208
209

ARGENTINA

AUSTRALIA

 ## BOTSWANA

BRAZIL

 ## CANADA

CARIBBEAN

CHILE

204
205
INDEX
206
207
208
209

INDEX

204
205
206

207
208
209

204
205
206
207

INDEX

208
209